READINGS ON

MEDEA

THE GREENHAVEN PRESS
Literary Companion
TO WORLD LITERATURE

READINGS ON

MEDEA

Don Nardo, *Book Editor*

David L. Bender, *Publisher*
Bruno Leone, *Executive Editor*
Bonnie Szumski, *Series Editor*

Greenhaven Press, Inc., San Diego, CA

Every effort has been made to trace the owners of copyrighted material. The articles in this volume may have been edited for content, length, and/or reading level. The titles have been changed to enhance the editorial purpose. Those interested in locating the original source will find the complete citation on the first page of each article.

Library of Congress Cataloging-in-Publication Data

Readings on Medea /Don Nardo, book editor.
    p. cm. — (The Greenhaven Press literary companion to world literature)
    Includes bibliographical references and index.
    ISBN 0-7377-0402-0 (pbk. : alk. paper) —
ISBN 0-7377-0403-9 (lib. bdg. : alk. paper)
    1. Euripides. Medea. 2. Medea (Greek mythology) in literature. 3. Women and literature—Greece. I. Nardo, Don, 1947–   II. Series.

PA3973.M4 R43 2001
882'.01—dc21

        00-026429

Cover photo: Musee des Beaux-Arts, Lille, France/A.K.G. Berlin/Superstock

Copyright © 2001 by Greenhaven Press, Inc.
PO Box 289009
San Diego, CA 92198-9009
Printed in the U.S.A.

66 *Surely, of all the creatures that have life and will, we women are the most wretched. . . . If a man grows tired of the company at home, he can go out, and find a cure for tediousness. We wives are forced to look to one man only. And, they tell us, we at home live free from danger, they go out to battle. Fools! I'd rather stand three times in the front line than bear one child.* 99

—Medea to the Chorus
in Euripides' *Medea*

CONTENTS

Chapter 1: The Plot, Structure, and Literary Devices of *Medea*

Chapter 2: Themes and Ideas Explored in the Play

Chapter 3: Medea and Other Major Characters

Chapter 4: Later Adaptations and Productions of *Medea*

FOREWORD

*"'Tis the good reader that
makes the good book."*

Ralph Waldo Emerson

The story's bare facts are simple: The captain, an old and scarred seafarer, walks with a peg leg made of whale ivory. He relentlessly drives his crew to hunt the world's oceans for the great white whale that crippled him. After a long search, the ship encounters the whale and a fierce battle ensues. Finally the captain drives his harpoon into the whale, but the harpoon line catches the captain about the neck and drags him to his death.

A simple story, a straightforward plot—yet, since the 1851 publication of Herman Melville's *Moby-Dick*, readers and critics have found many meanings in the struggle between Captain Ahab and the whale. To some, the novel is a cautionary tale that depicts how Ahab's obsession with revenge leads to his insanity and death. Others believe that the whale represents the unknowable secrets of the universe and that Ahab is a tragic hero who dares to challenge fate by attempting to discover this knowledge. Perhaps Melville intended Ahab as a criticism of Americans' tendency to become involved in well-intentioned but irrational causes. Or did Melville model Ahab after himself, letting his fictional character express his anger at what he perceived as a cruel and distant god?

Although literary critics disagree over the meaning of *Moby-Dick*, readers do not need to choose one particular interpretation in order to gain an understanding of Melville's novel. Instead, by examining various analyses, they can gain numerous insights into the issues that lie under the surface of the basic plot. Studying the writings of literary critics can also aid readers in making their own assessments of *Moby-Dick* and other literary works and in developing analytical thinking skills.

The Greenhaven Literary Companion Series was created with these goals in mind. Designed for young adults, this unique anthology series provides an engaging and comprehensive introduction to literary analysis and criticism. The essays included in the Literary Companion Series are chosen for their accessibility to a young adult audience and are expertly edited in consideration of both the reading and comprehension levels of this audience. In addition, each essay is introduced by a concise summation that presents the contributing writer's main themes and insights. Every anthology in the Literary Companion Series contains a varied selection of critical essays that cover a wide time span and express diverse views. Wherever possible, primary sources are represented through excerpts from authors' notebooks, letters, and journals and through contemporary criticism.

Each title in the Literary Companion Series pays careful consideration to the historical context of the particular author or literary work. In-depth biographies and detailed chronologies reveal important aspects of authors' lives and emphasize the historical events and social milieu that influenced their writings. To facilitate further research, every anthology includes primary and secondary source bibliographies of articles and/or books selected for their suitability for young adults. These engaging features make the Greenhaven Literary Companion series ideal for introducing students to literary analysis in the classroom or as a library resource for young adults researching the world's great authors and literature.

Exceptional in its focus on young adults, the Greenhaven Literary Companion Series strives to present literary criticism in a compelling and accessible format. Every title in the series is intended to spark readers' interest in leading American and world authors, to help them broaden their understanding of literature, and to encourage them to formulate their own analyses of the literary works that they read. It is the editors' hope that young adult readers will find these anthologies to be true companions in their study of literature.

INTRODUCTION

The reader might well ask why he or she should bother studying Euripides' *Medea*, a play written over twenty-four hundred years ago. What qualities could such a presumably antiquated work possess to justify his or her attention? And what possible relevance could its characters and situations have to modern life and society?

The answer to these questions is that, despite the passage of so many centuries, Euripides' famous play about the murderous rage of a woman scorned is not in the least antiquated. First, the society in which he wrote bore a number of striking similarities to that of the United States and several other modern Western industrialized nations. Fifth-century B.C. Athens and modern society are both characterized by a strong emphasis on the individual and his or her needs, desires, and beliefs. Both also feature an unprecedented degree of freedom of speech and the tendency of artists in the popular media to exploit it by exploring and sometimes questioning and criticizing traditional social values and institutions. In addition, of all the classical Greek dramatists Euripides was the foremost social questioner and critic. In his own time, he was a bit of a rebel and some of his countrymen probably saw him as a subversive influence; yet these very qualities make him, from our vantage, the most modern dramatist of the ancient world. "Euripides is closer to us [than other ancient playwrights]," remarks noted scholar D.W. Lucas, "and his troubles and difficulties have something in common with our own."[1]

One particularly modern quality of Euripides' work is his attempt to explore and dramatically exploit the social and psychological problems of real people. Indeed, he was the first known artist to do so. For instance, though the title character of *Medea* is decidedly larger-than-life and resorts to what most people would view as extreme actions, women throughout the ages can readily identify with her dilemma.

For his own selfish reasons, her husband, Jason, has suddenly abandoned her for another woman. In one magnificently worded speech after another, she expresses the same feelings of helplessness, indignation, and rage felt by countless women who have been unfairly dominated, abused, and/or dismissed by men. Most rejected wives would not kill their own children to get revenge on their husbands, as Medea does. Yet all women, and many men as well, fully understand her plight, her anger, and her desire to punish the man who has wronged her. In this respect, the play remains every bit as fresh and vital as when it was first written.

Other reasons that *Medea* deserves continued attention and study are the excellence of its execution and sheer beauty of its language. Voicing the general consensus of scholars and teachers, one of their number calls it "one of the greatest of all plays,"[2] and another "a brilliant intellectual achievement."[3] In addition, there is the continuing attraction of the raw power of the title role for the great actresses of each new generation. "The desire to produce this one of Euripides' dramas," says University of Florida scholar Karelisa V. Hartigan, "must rest, ultimately, on its theatricality and the strong character of Medea herself; her great scenes are a challenge for any actress."[4]

The essays selected for the Greenhaven Literary Companion to Euripides' *Medea* provide teachers and students with a wide range of information and opinion about the play and its author's style, themes, and outlook on the human condition. All of the authors of the essays are or were (until their deaths) professors at leading colleges and universities, noted scholars specializing in ancient Greek literature and drama, or widely respected authorities on Euripides and his works. Among this companion volume's several special features: each of the essays explains or discusses in detail a specific, narrowly focused topic; the introduction to each essay previews the main points; and inserts interspersed within the essays serve as examples of ideas expressed by the authors, offer supplementary information, and/or add authenticity and color. Above all, this companion book is designed to enhance the reader's understanding and enjoyment of a timeless, classic tale of betrayal, anger, and revenge, one that remains strangely compelling even though its climax continues both to shock and disturb people. As Medea herself says, "To say what I have to say will ease my heart; to hear it said will make you wince."[5]

NOTES

1. D.W. Lucas, *The Greek Tragic Poets.* New York: W.W. Norton, 1959, p.243.
2. John Ferguson, *A Companion to Greek Tragedy.* Austin: University of Texas Press, 1972, pp.247–48.
3. Peter D. Arnott, trans. and ed., *Three Greek Plays for the Theater.* Bloomington: Indiana University Press, 1961, p.23.
4. Karelisa V. Hartigan, *Greek Tragedy on the American Stage: Ancient Drama in the Commercial Theater, 1882–1994.* Westport, CT: Greenwood Press, 1995, p.48.
5. Euripides, *Medea* 470–471, in Philip Vellacott, trans., *Euripides: Medea and Other Plays.* New York: Penguin Books, 1963, p.31.

EURIPIDES AND *MEDEA*

One of the four masters of fifth-century B.C. Athenian drama, Euripides was most likely born about 485 B.C. on the Athenian-controlled island of Salamis (situated a few miles southwest of Athens). The narrow strait adjoining the island was the site of the renowned Greek naval victory over the Persians, fought on or about September 20, 480. And the famous first-century B.C. biographer Plutarch and some other ancient authorities report that Euripides came into the world on the very day of the great battle. However, this is probably a later rumor or fabrication, one example of the common ancient practice of glorifying notable figures of the past by associating their births or deaths with momentous earthly or cosmic events.

Very little is known about Euripides' childhood and young manhood except that his father's name was Mnesarchides (also the name of one of Euripides' own sons) and his mother was called Clito. The most complete surviving source about the playwright, a short anonymous work generally referred to as the *Life,* claims that as a boy he played a prominent role in some religious festivals, bearing a sacred torch in one of them. If true, this would suggest that his parents were well-to-do or at least prominent and highly respected members of the community. The *Life* also says that young Euripides took part in athletics, excelling in boxing and the pankration (a rough-and-tumble combination of boxing and wrestling). In addition, he may have started his career as a painter, taking up dramatics later. Perhaps he was bitten by the theater bug while painting backgrounds on the scene building (*skene*) that stood behind the round acting area (orchestra) in Athens's Theater of Dionysus. "It may well be," comments his modern biographer, William N. Bates, "that the vividness of some of his descriptions is due in part to his experience as a painter."[1]

Of one aspect of Euripides' early life there can be no doubt. That is the special, indeed one could even say unique, nature of the society and age in which he was fortunate to be raised.

In the fifth century B.C., Athens was the largest, most populous, and most politically and culturally influential city-state in all of Greece. And its achievements in that age still stand as a monument to the highest spirit of human talent and creative endeavor. "The days of the youth and early manhood of Euripides," writes noted scholar Rex Warner,

> were passed in what most Athenians would have regarded as a blaze of patriotic splendor. We, looking back on those times, can see them as a unique period in the history of the world, a period in which were laid the foundations our present-day civilization. These years saw the invention of drama, the fine flowering of sculpture and architecture, the foundations laid of law and politics, of science and philosophy. But all of these were merely aspects of a way of life achieved miraculously, it seems to us who look back on it all, by a few generations of men. In ways unparalleled before in history men sought to understand, to explain and, at least in so far as human relationships are concerned, to reshape the world in which they lived. They looked at everything in heaven and earth with strangely unprejudiced eyes, and from what they saw they made new products of theory, imagination, and behavior.[2]

A STRING OF MASTERPIECES

Euripides began writing plays during the very years that Athens was building its short-lived maritime empire, expanding the freedoms of its democracy (the world's first, created in the last years of the preceding century), and beginning to erect temples that would awe later generations. According to one ancient source, he first competed in Athens's great dramatics festival and competition—the City Dionysia—in 455 B.C. Another source dates his first victory in the competition to about 441. In all, he supposedly wrote some eighty-eight plays. But only nineteen have survived. These are *Alcestis* (438), *Medea* (431), *Children of Heracles* (ca.430), *Hippolytus* (428), *Andromache* (ca.426), *Hecuba* (ca.424), *The Suppliant Women* (ca.422), *Heracles* (ca.422-417), *Madness of Heracles* (ca.420-417), *Electra* (ca.417-413), *Ion* (ca.417), *The Trojan Women* (415), *Iphigenia in Taurus* (ca.414), *The Phoenician Women* (ca.412-408), *Helen* (412), *Orestes* (408), *The Bacchae* (405), *Iphigenia in Aulus* (ca.405), and *The Cyclops* (date unknown).

Incredibly, this string of masterpieces, beside which the works of most playwrights pale, regularly faced stiff competition and their author most often finished second or third in the dramatics competitions. In fact, Euripides won first place in the City Dionysia only five times and was far less popular in his own day than either of the other two giants of Athenian tragedy—Aeschylus and Sophocles, both his seniors. (Sophocles reportedly won first prize at the City Dionysia eighteen times and never placed lower than second.)

This difference between the public perception and popularity of Euripides and that of his rivals stemmed partly from the fact that his plays often questioned and criticized traditional and widely accepted social values. By contrast, the characters and situations in the works of Aeschylus and Sophocles tended to uphold and venerate traditional values, especially those that emanated from the gods. Euripides suggested, for example, that life consists of a series of random events, so that the world operates more by chance than under the influence of the gods and preordained fate. In this view, human beings are just as concerned as the gods, or even more concerned, with establishing moral values.

Moreover, Euripides often makes the gods behave badly in his plays, something rarely seen in the works of his contempories.[5] In *Hippolytus,* for example, Aphrodite, goddess of love, savagely strikes out at the title character simply because of her wounded vanity. In *Helen,* the title character never makes it to Troy, where traditional legends claimed the Trojan prince Paris carried her, igniting the famous Trojan War, which her husband and other Greek kings fought to get her back. Instead, the goddess Hera (Zeus's wife) created a "phantom" Helen; and it was this phantom that was at Troy, while the real Helen spent the whole ten years of the war in Egypt. Euripides therefore implies that the gods are cruel deceivers who allow thousands to suffer and die for something they think exists but in reality does not. Still another example is his play *Ion,* in which Apollo, god of light and healing, rapes and abandons the heroine, Creusa. In the course of the play she loudly denounces the deity, which surely made some Athenian playgoers cringe.

These and other examples of Euripides' unsavory characterizations of the Greek gods have led some modern observers to conclude that he must have rejected their very existence and was therefore an atheist. This is unlikely, however. The City Dionysia and other dramatics competitions were, first and foremost, religious festivals that included much overt and sincere prayer and sacrifice. It is hardly likely that Athenian authorities and audiences would have allowed an avowed atheist to defame the gods repeatedly in public. The truth is that most of the plots of the plays presented at these festivals derived from mythology. And in these traditional stories the gods sometimes did behave rather badly. The difference between Euripides and most other playwrights was that they usually did not emphasize or criticize such divine missteps, whereas he did. This alone was enough to shock and disturb many of his contemporaries and earn him a reputation for flirting with impiety (lack of religious reverence).

IDEAS AHEAD OF THEIR TIME

Euripides also boldly questioned some of the leading social and political conventions of his day. Although Athens was a democracy, and a very open one at that, most of its leaders were still drawn from the upper classes, for the families of the old aristocracy still held much power and social prestige. As noted scholar D.W. Lucas asks, did these people of wealth and privilege "have an innate fitness to rule, or had they merely learned what, given time and opportunity anyone else could learn?"[4] Euripides pointed out the uncertainty and hollowness of such class distinctions in his *Electra.* "There is no clear sign to tell the quality of a man," the hero Orestes proclaims.

> Nature and place turn vice and virtue upside down. I've seen a noble father breed a worthless son, and good sons come of evil parents; a starved soul housed in a rich man's palace, a great heart dressed in rags. By what sign, then, shall one tell good from bad? By wealth? Wealth's a false standard. By possessing nothing, then? No; poverty is a disease; and want itself trains men in crime. Or must I look to see how men behave in battle? When you're watching your enemy's spear you don't know who's brave, who's a coward. The best way is to judge each man as you find him; there's no rule.[5]

This is an extremely democratic sentiment because it presupposes that anyone, given the right opportunities, might be fit to rule. It explains why the philosopher Socrates, who disapproved of democracy, was said to have walked out of a performance of one of Euripides' plays. It also provides another example of the playwright being far ahead of his time and anticipating modern ideas about social and political equality.

Another aspect of Euripides' modernity was his use of what we today would call realism. The plays of Aeschylus and Sophocles are, for the most part, very formal and stylistic in their presentation. They usually deal with larger-than-life heroes and heroines, depict their legendary deeds and interactions with the gods, and/or explore how they and those around them come to grief because of tragic character flaws. Ordinary people, such as messengers and servants, play only minor supporting roles in these dramas. Euripides' plays also have their mythological heroes and gods and, like all Greek drama, were staged in a stylistic way—i.e., with masked actors, choruses that sang and/or recited the lines in unison, and so forth. But in a majority of his works he showed characters, even high-born ones, wrestling with the emotions, passions, and personal problems of ordinary people in realistic ways.

In *Helen,* for example, Menelaus, king of Sparta, appears onstage in rags after being shipwrecked. This likely shocked Athenian audiences, who were used to the formal convention of kings being well-dressed no matter what the situation. And in both *Hippolytus* and *Medea,* leading female characters talk about being in love, as well as about the pitfalls and abuses that sometimes accompany it, in an open manner, as an Athenian woman might when complaining to her husband or sister. This sort of candor by women was seen as improper in a public forum and Euripides was often criticized for a lack of dignity. Thus, while the stories he told were based in familiar mythological territory, his mythical characters had, in Rex Warner's words, "become reborn as contemporary human beings, each of whom was an individual in his or her own right."[6]

THE SENSELESSNESS OF WAR

Another way that Euripides depicted the human condition in a realistic way was to show the cruel and unfair ways that war affects ordinary people. Perhaps more than any other ancient writer, he was concerned with not only the destruction and waste, but also the human suffering caused by war. The latter part of Euripides' career took place during the disastrous Peloponnesian War, which ravaged Greece from 431 to 404 B.C. and ended with Athens' defeat at the hands of its arch-rival, Sparta. In his *Trojan Women* (produced in 415), a grim and moving hymn to the senselessness of war, as well as in other works, he made it abundantly clear that ordinary people, including women and slaves, could suffer from war's ravages just as much as the kings and their generals. Partly for this, in his *Poetics* the famous philosopher Aristotle (384–323 B.C.) calls Euripides the most skilled of the tragic poets at arousing emotions like pity and fear.

Perhaps fortunately for Euripides, he did not live long enough to see his country defeated and its cherished democracy dismantled by the enemy. In 408, some four years before the great war's conclusion, he accepted an invitation to live and write at the court of Macedonia (a kingdom in extreme northern Greece). And in 406 he died there at about the age of seventy-nine. When the news reached Athens, just before the opening of that year's City Dionysia, his colleague Sophocles honored his memory by dressing his own actors in mourning clothes during the public procession that preceded the contests. The Athenians requested that the body be returned to their city; but for reasons unknown the Macedonians refused and buried the playwright in their own soil. In the century that followed, Euripides, who had struggled for the acceptance and acclaim of audiences in his own time, came into his own and his works came to be read and acted far more than those of all the other dramatists combined.

THE EVENTS AND THEMES OF *MEDEA*

It is unknown which of Euripides' plays was most popular in the centuries immediately following his death. But it is fairly certain that *Medea* has been the most popular and most often performed in modern times. This popularity is due to certain qualities, features, and themes the work possesses that make it extremely appealing to readers and theater audiences alike. First, the play deals with themes universal to every society and age, among them failed marriage, men's mistreatment of women, betrayal, jealousy, deceit, revenge, and murder.

As the play opens, Medea, the sorceress who helped the hero Jason acquire the fabulous Golden Fleece in his most famous adventure, has just been betrayed by him. Though they have been married for some time and have two children, he has consented to marry the daughter of Creon, king of Corinth. Consumed with jealousy and rage, the scorned woman plots her revenge. For a while, she pretends to accept Jason's actions so as to divert suspicion from her deadly plans, which include the painful death of the princess. Having accomplished this deed, she turns on her own children, killing them in an attempt to hurt Jason. Thus, her desire for revenge is so great that it overpowers her normal maternal instincts. Before Jason or anyone else can bring her to justice, Medea escapes to Athens, where the local king gives her refuge.

These horrifying events unfold rapidly and relentlessly. From Medea's own words as she plots the murders, the audience knows well in advance that the princess and children are in mortal danger. And as the danger mounts, the hope that she will change her mind or that somehow the victims, especially the children, will somehow escape causes ten-sions to rise in a terrible crescendo. This gives the play a highly theatrical, dramatic, and compelling tone and feeling.

Another compelling aspect of the play is that it deals with a woman who says and does things that women traditionally do not say and do. As in his plays *Hippolytus, Hecuba,* and *Andromache,* in *Medea* Euripides depicts a woman driven to or caught up in violence and tragedy by extreme circumstances. This then revolutionary vision of women became one of the playwright's hallmarks, in fact. He "produced a series of tragic studies in womanhood which appalled and delighted his audiences," remarked the late, great scholar C.M. Bowra.

> [By] overriding the conventional view of women, he created something entirely new in these intimate, accurate, merciless and yet completely sympathetic studies of violent lost souls. . . . In each case the conflict in the chief character is mirrored in the external conflict round them, and each plot is concerned with the clash of competing wills and even of irreconcilable characters [those who can never see eye to eye or make peace with each other]. . . . In each case the issue is painful, and unless the gods intervene, there is no solution but disaster and death.[7]

A CITY BLESSED BY THE GODS

In *Medea,* of course, the disaster and death take the form of child-murder. When the play was first produced in 431 B.C., Athenian audiences were no doubt just as disturbed as modern ones are at the spectacle of a mother slaughtering her own children. Today, spectators either find the title character evil, despicable, and completely unsympathetic for this bloody act, or else they sympathize with her plight and understand her rage, even while admitting that she goes too far in killing the children. The original Athenian audiences, however, perceived another dimension of the situation that modern audiences usually overlook. This was that Medea was a foreigner and a non-Greek and therefore a "barbarian," the term the Greeks used to describe non–Greek-speaking peoples. The idea that Greeks, in particular Athenians, were more civilized, and therefore superior, to barbarians was a common theme of Athenian art and literature. And the playwright could not resist inserting in *Medea* a beautiful hymn of praise to his native city. When it becomes clear that Medea will seek asylum in Athens after doing her dirty deeds, the chorus wonders whether so civilized a people will be able to accept and give sustenance to a murderess. "Children of blessed gods," the chorus sings, the Athenians grew from holy soil unscorched by invasion. Among the glories of knowledge their souls are pastured; they walk always with grace under the sparkling sky. There long ago, they say, was born golden-haired Harmony, created by the nine virgin Muses [goddesses of the creative arts]. . . . They say that Aphrodite dips her cup in the clear stream of the lovely Cephisus [the main river in the plain in which Athens lies]; it is she who breathes over the land the breath of gentle honey-laden winds; her flowing locks she crowns with a diadem [crown] of sweet-scented roses, and sends the Loves to be enthroned beside Knowledge, and with her to create excellence in every art. Then how will such a city, watered by sacred rivers. . . welcome you, the child-killer whose presence is pollution [religious taint]?[8]

Euripides develops this theme of civilization versus barbarism in *Medea* in two ways. On the one hand, the leading character is a barbarian princess who marries a Greek. His audiences would have seen Medea as capable of killing her own children, something no Athenian would even consider, in part because she is the product of a primitive culture in which human life has less value. At the same time, Euripides makes things more complex and interesting by, in a way, turning this fairly simple idea, one biased heavily in favor of the Greeks, upside-down. Although Medea, the foreign sorceress, is wild, dangerous, and not to be trusted, she is still, in the playwright's eyes, to be pitied for her husband's abandonment of her. Indeed, though her murders of the princess and children are extreme reactions, Euripides seems to feel that some kind of extreme reaction is justified on her part. And he makes her strength and spirit, even when used for ill, seem admirable. This can be inferred in part from his portrayal of Jason. Much unlike the typical Greek hero and not at all a fitting representative of civilized Greek culture, he is pictured in the play as weak and unworthy. Classical scholars Victor Hanson and John Heath call him a "simpleton" who is

either unaware or deathly afraid of her [Medea's] touched genius and indomitable spirit. In short, there is no more dislikable figure in classical literature than Medea's husband, Jason, whom Euripides caricatures as the typical couch-lounging lout, pouting and whining through his pathetic midlife crisis. It is the foreign-born Medea, not the sniveling Greek Jason, who eloquently decries the inequities of Athenian life [primarily the second-class status of women].[9]

MEDEA IN THE CORINTHIAN LEGENDS

Euripides' highly personalized characterizations of Medea and Jason illustrate well that, though he based this and his other stories on existing myths, he did not shrink from altering the legends for dramatic effect. In fact, it appears that he changed or added several important elements in Medea's story. In the legends of the Corinthians themselves, for instance, Medea was more than just a barbarian princess whom Jason brought to Greece. According to a local Corinthian myth, in the dim past the sun-god Helios arranged for his two sons, Aloeus and Aeetes, to divide and rule the kingdom of Corinth. Aeetes took charge of the city itself; but later he journeyed to faraway Colchis, on the shores of the Black Sea, leaving a man named Bounos to rule Corinth. After several generations had passed, one of Aeetes' descendants, also of that name, sired Medea. And when she grew to womanhood, the Corinthians called on her to return and become their queen. In this scenario, the Corinthian throne was rightfully hers by inheritance and Jason became ruler of Corinth only because he had married her after their adventures with the Golden Fleece.

It seems that Medea's murder of the children is also an invention of the playwright. In the Corinthian myths, after Medea did the goddess Hera a favor, Hera promised to make her children immortal. But before the process was complete, a group of Corinthians killed the children to punish Medea for leaving the city and seeking sanctuary in a temple of Hera. To cover up their terrible deed, the murderers spread the rumor that Medea had killed her own children; and Euripides apparently saw the dramatic possibilities of this idea and made it the centerpiece of his play. In this way, he took an otherwise obscure legendary princess and transformed her into a ferocious, often frightening, and decidedly larger-than-life character who remains one of the great heroines of the tragic stage.

NOTES

1. William N. Bates, *Euripides: A Student of Human Nature.* New York: Russell and Russell, 1969, p.6.
2. Rex Warner, trans., *Three Great Plays of Euripides.* New York: New American Library, 1958, pp.vii–viii.
3. A notable exception is Aeschylus's *Prometheus Bound,* in which Zeus, leader of the gods, is portrayed as cruel, arbitrary, and unjust in his punishment of the heroic Prometheus. However, this admission that Zeus is far from perfect is less Aeschylus's personal observation and more a part of the way the Greeks viewed the gods—as beings far more powerful than humans, but having some of the same emotions and character flaws as humans.

4. D.W. Lucas, *The Greek Tragic Poets.* New York: W.W. Norton, 1959, p.239.
5. Euripides, *Electra* 368-379, in Philip Vellacott, trans., *Euripides: Medea and Other Plays.* New York: Penguin Books, 1963, pp.117–18.
6. Warner, *Three Great Plays of Euripides,* pp.xvi-xvii.
7. C.M. Bowra, *Ancient Greek Literature.* New York: Oxford University Press, 1960, pp.111–12.
8. Euripides, *Medea* 826-838, in Vellacott, *Euripides: Medea and Other Plays,* pp.42–43.
9. Victor D. Hanson and John Heath, *Who Killed Homer? The Demise of Classical Education and the Recovery of Greek Wisdom.* New York: Free Press, 1998, p.103.

CHARACTERS

Medea. A princess of the faraway kingdom of Colchis (on the shores of the Black Sea), who settled in the Greek city of Corinth ten years ago with her husband, Jason. She has been recently surprised and enraged to hear that he is abandoning her for another woman.

Jason. The renowned Greek hero who sailed to Colchis on his ship, the *Argo,* and successfully captured the fabulous Golden Fleece. He recently consented to marry the daughter of the king of Corinth.

Creon. The king of Corinth, who has offered the hand of his daughter in marriage to Jason.

Medea's two sons. Completely innocent, they are about to become the unfortunate victims of their father's infidelity and their mother's anger and vengeance.

Nurse to Medea's sons. When the nurse hears that Medea and the children have been banished from Corinth, she fears the severity of Medea's wrath.

Tutor to Medea's sons. He eventually brings Medea the good news that the King has decided not to banish the children.

Messenger. He arrives from the palace to describe the hideous death of the king and princess.

Aegeus. The king of the neighboring city of Athens, he agrees to give Medea sanctuary after she is banished from Corinth.

Chorus. A group of Corinthian women who stand by watching events unfold. They comment on these events and also converse with some of the main characters.

THE PLAY IN MYTHIC CONTEXT: MEDEA'S AND JASON'S EARLIER ADVENTURES

At the point in Medea's life at which Euripides chose to begin his famous play about her, she and Jason have known each other for some time and shared in some daring adventures. From a chronological standpoint, the earliest depiction of Medea in ancient Greek mythology appears in the popular legend of Jason and the quest for the Golden Fleece. The classical Greeks (ca. fifth-fourth centuries B.C.) held that Jason's adventure, involving his ship, the *Argo*, and his crew, the Argonauts, took place in the generation directly preceding the Trojan War. This semi-legendary sacking of the city of Troy (in Asia Minor, what is now Turkey) by the Greeks was traditionally dated to about 1250–1200 B.C. So the voyage of the *Argo* and the exploits of Jason and Medea supposedly took place sometime in the thirteenth century B.C.

Several ancient writers produced versions of the quest for the Fleece, among them the fifth-century B.C. Greek poet, Pindar, in one of his *Odes;* and the third-century B.C. Greek writer, Apollonius of Rhodes, in his almost six-thousand-line epic poem, the *Argonautica.* This work is particularly noteworthy because it was the first major attempt to portray romantic love from a woman's point of view, in this case Medea's. The first-century A.D. Roman epic poet Valerius Flaccus also wrote an *Argonautica* that has survived.

THE ONE-SANDALED MAN

The story of the quest for the Golden Fleece, in which Medea and Jason first meet, begins not long after an oracle (a priestess who spoke for the gods) had delivered a prophecy to Pelias, king of the powerful city of Jolcos (in Thessaly, in central Greece). The oracle warned Pelias, who had earlier usurped the throne from his uncle, that he should beware of any stranger who arrived in Jolcos wearing only one sandal. Such a man, said the priestess, would cause Pelias to lose both his throne and his life. And it came to pass that just such a one-sandaled man appeared at the palace, having lost a sandal while crossing a flooded stream. He informed Pelias that he was his cousin Jason, son of the rightful king, and that he had come to claim his birthright and to bring enlightened rule to Jolcos, which Pelias had administered harshly.

Pelias deviously pretended to agree with Jason's claim to the throne, but secretly he plotted to rid himself of the young man. "You shall become king of Jolcos indeed," Pelias told Jason. "But first you must accomplish a special task. I am continually vexed by a spirit who bids me to bring the fabulous Fleece of the legendary Golden Ram back to Jolcos, its rightful home. At the moment, the Fleece hangs in a tree in the faraway land of Colchis and since I am too old and weak to make the journey, you must do so. When you return with the Fleece, I swear by Father Zeus that I will abdicate and make you king." This was a lie, of course. Pelias knew full well that the voyage to Colchis was long and extremely treacherous and that in all likelihood Jason would never return.

But Jason felt confident that he could bring back the Fleece. To do so, he realized, he would need a special ship and, under the direction of the goddess Athena, the master shipbuilder Argus constructed the mighty *Argo*. According to Valerius Flaccus's account,

> a large gathering of men worked busily. At the same time . . .
> a grove of trees had been felled on all sides and the stores
> were resounding with the steady blows of the double-edged
> ax. Already Argus was cutting pines with the thin blade of a
> saw, and the sides of the ship were being fitted together. . . .
> Planks [were] being softened over a slow fire until they bent
> to the proper shape. The oars had been fashioned and Pallas
> Athena was seeking out a yardarm for the sail-carrying mast.
> When the ship stood finished, strong enough to plow through
> the pathless sea. . . Argus added varied ornamental paint-
> ings.[1]

Such a superior ship needed a superior crew and Jason soon gathered together many of the strongest, ablest, and noblest men of Greece. Among them were the mighty hero Heracles, accompanied by his faithful armor-bearer Hylas; the master musician and singer Orpheus; the warrior Peleus (father of Achilles); Zeus's twin sons Castor and Polydeuces (the Roman Pollux); and many others.

THE DANGEROUS VOYAGE TO COLCHIS

Having stored sufficient provisions, Jason and his Argonauts finally embarked and sailed north. It was not long before they encountered their first setback, which took place near a pleasant bay where they had stopped for rest and exercise. As the noted nineteenth-century classical scholar Charles Kingsley told it:

> Heracles went away into the woods, bow in hand, to hunt wild deer; and Hylas the fair boy slipped away after him, and followed him by stealth, until he lost himself among the glens, and sat down weary to rest himself by the side of a lake; and there the water nymphs came up to look at him, and loved him, and carried him down under the lake to be their playfellow, forever happy and young. And Heracles sought for him in vain, shouting his name till all the mountains rang; but Hylas never heard him down under the sparkling lake. So while Heracles wandered searching for him, a fair breeze sprang up, and Heracles was nowhere to be found; and the *Argo* sailed away, and Heracles was left behind.[2]

Thus, Heracles missed the Argonauts' subsequent adventures. These included narrowly making it through a channel bordered by the dreaded Clashing Rocks, which perpetually smashed together, destroying anything caught between them; and passing perilously near the country of the Amazons (daughters of the war god Ares), a tribe of fierce women warriors. They also sailed past the great rock on which the god Prometheus lay chained (as a punishment for angering Zeus) and heard the flapping of the wings of the giant eagle that pecked and tore at his liver.[3]

In one particularly exotic and dangerous episode, the Argonauts tangled with the terrifying Harpies, flying creatures endowed with pointed beaks and claws and a sickening stench. Jason and his men found an old man named Phineus, who was so starved and emaciated that all that was left of him was quite literally skin and bones. Apollo had once granted Phineus the gift of prophecy; but Zeus disapproved of humans knowing what he was going to do next and inflicted a punishment on the man. Every time Phineus began to eat a meal, the Harpies, sometimes called "Zeus's Hounds," would swoop down and cover his food with their stench, making it too disgusting to consume. In a courageous effort, some of the Argonauts succeeded in driving the Harpies away, so that they never again bothered poor Phineus.

FIRE-BREATHING BULLS AND DRAGONS' TEETH

Eventually, Jason and his crew reached the land of Colchis, on the far end of the Axine, or Unfriendly Sea.[4] There, they asked the local king, Aeetes, to give them the Golden Fleece, in exchange for which they would do him some important service, such as fighting his enemies. But Aeetes did not like foreigners and in any case was not about to give up the Fleece, so he concocted a plan that would surely result in Jason's death. No one could take the Fleece, Aeetes claimed, unless he first proved his courage through a formidable challenge. He would have to yoke two fearsome fire-breathing bulls and use them to plow dragons' teeth into the earth. These seeds would quickly grow into a multitude of armed warriors, whom he would have to defeat.

At first, it seemed to Jason that no mortal man could pass such a test. But he soon received some unexpected and formidable aid. The goddess Hera, who wanted Jason's quest to succeed, convinced Aphrodite to send her own son Eros (the Roman Cupid) to Colchis. Eros caused King Aeetes's daughter, Medea, almost instantly to fall in love with Jason; and indeed, her love became so strong that she was willing to betray her own father for this Greek stranger. Medea, who possessed knowledge of sorcery, met Jason in secret and gave him a vile containing a magic drug. In Apollonius's version of the story, she gave Jason these instructions:

> At dawn, steep this drug in water, strip off naked, and rub it all over your body like oil: within it there'll be great strength and unlimited prowess—it's not men you'd think of matching yourself with, but the immortal gods. On top of this, see that your spear and shield are sprinkled, and your sword too: then you'll be proof against the spear-points of the earthborn men, against the irresistible onrush of flame from the deadly bulls.[5]

And sure enough, covered in this special ointment, Jason was able to yoke the bulls, defeat the seed-warriors, and thereby to pass the test. Aeetes still did not want to give up the Fleece. But with more help from Medea, Jason managed to get past the huge serpent that guarded the Fleece and to spirit the prize out of Colchis. As Jason and Medea made their escape in the *Argo*, she cut up the body of her own brother, whom she had just murdered to facilitate the getaway, and threw the pieces into the water. Just as she had hoped, when her father's ships gave chase, their crews stopped frequently to collect the gory fragments for a proper burial. That way, the *Argo* was able to gain time and make it back to Greece with its prize.

MEDEA AND JASON IN GREECE

Once the Argonauts returned to Greece, they disbanded and some went on to further adventures of their own. Some had sons, who, when they grew into young men, joined the great Greek expedition against Troy that ended with that city's destruction. For example, Peleus's son, Achilles, became the war's most famous hero. Meanwhile, to give thanks to the gods for his safe return, Jason dedicated the *Argo* to the sea god, Poseidon. Jason also dutifully presented the captured fleece to King Pelias, expecting that the old man would keep his end of the bargain and abdicate his throne in favor of Jason. But Pelias refused to fulfill his earlier promise to abdicate. Instead, he continued to cheat Jason out of his rights as the true heir to Jolcos's throne. While the dispute dragged on and on, Jason and Medea had two children together in Jolcos.

Finally, quite fed up with Pelias's deceit, Medea decided to help Jason attain both the throne and revenge on Pelias. She took the king's three daughters aside and told them a fantastic tale. "Your father is an old man who will, no doubt, die in the near future," she said. "Wouldn't you like to see him recapture his youth and reign for many more decades?" The princesses quickly agreed that they would eagerly welcome such a turn of events, although they could scarcely believe that such a thing was possible. Medea assured them that it was indeed possible. She then proceeded to convince the gullible young women that if they killed Pelias, cut him into pieces, and treated the pieces with magic herbs and spells (which Medea would supply), he would suddenly be rejuvenated as a young man.[6] Believing this lie, the princesses followed Medea's instructions and slaughtered their father. The result, as Medea had planned, was Pelias's grisly and very permanent death, not his resurrection.

Medea's devious plan succeeded in accomplishing only one of its intended aims, however. Jason had indeed achieved revenge on Pelias. But the young hero did not attain the throne of Jolcos, as he had desired. Pelias's son, Acastus, branded both Jason and Medea murderers and drove them and their young children from the city. The exiled family journeyed southward to the prosperous city of Corinth. Here, to Medea's surprise and dismay, Jason turned on her. He rejected her as his wife and married the daughter of Creon, king of Corinth, perhaps, as he claimed, to put himself in a better economic and political position and thereby to have a chance to inherit the city's throne someday. It is at this fateful juncture, with Medea fuming with rage over Jason's betrayal, that the action of Euripides' great play about her begins.

NOTES

1. Valerius Flaccus, *Argonautica,* excerpted in Rhoda A. Hendricks, trans., *Classical Gods and Heroes.* New York: Morrow, 1974, p.183.
2. Charles Kingsley, *The Heroes.* Santa Rosa, CA: Classics Press, 1968, pp.73–74.
3. According to one of the main myths about Prometheus, Zeus punished him for giving the secret of fire to humans, which Zeus had earlier forbidden him to do. As part of the punishment, each day the eagle fed on Prometheus's liver and each night the organ grew back so that the hideous process could begin again.
4. This was the early Greek name for what we now know as the Black Sea. The later classical Greeks, having explored and colonized it, called it the Euxine, or Friendly Sea.
5. Apollonius of Rhodes, *Argonautica.* Trans. Peter Green, excerpted in Bernard Knox, ed., *The Norton Book of Classical Literature.* New York: W.W. Norton, 1993, pp.544–45.
6. In some versions of the story, Medea demonstrates for the princesses the use of the magic herbs and spells by turning an old ram into a fluffy young lamb.

CHAPTER 1

The Plot, Structure, and Literary Devices of Medea

READINGS ON
MEDEA

The Story Told in *Medea*

Siegfried Melchinger

The following synopsis of the action of Euripides' most famous play is by the noted German scholar and expert on Euripides and his works, Siegfried Melchinger. He begins with a brief recap of how Jason brought Medea back from Colchis (on the far shores of the Black Sea) to the Greek city of Jolcos (or Iolcos), and then proceeds to outline the play's plot, discussing the motivations of the characters where necessary. Melchinger also mentions the *deus ex machina*, or "god from the machine," the visually effective stage and literary device used in the climax. The "machine" consisted of a crane that allowed actors playing gods, heroes, or others to be suspended high in the air over the stage.

Jason, the hero of the legend of the Argonauts, has carried off the golden fleece, famed in mythology, from Colchis on the Black Sea. As reward for this feat he was to get the throne usurped by his father's half-brother, Pelias. He could never have succeeded in stealing this prize in that distant land if he had not had the help there of the king's daughter, the princess Medea. She fell madly in love with him, and with her magic potions she put the dragons who guarded the treasure to sleep. Then, by murdering her brother, she made Jason's escape possible and fled with him.

After adventurous travels, Jason brought the fleece home to Iolcus, where he expected it would help him to obtain his father's throne. In spite of his hopes, the throne was denied him. To aid him, Medea devised a stratagem. Deceived by Medea's promise that she could put Pelias together and make him young again by the use of her magic mixtures, Pelias's own daughters killed him and cut him into pieces.

Pelias's son now drove Jason and Medea with their children out of Iolcus. Becoming refugees, they found temporary asylum in Corinth, where King Creon has a daughter but no son. Jason has wooed and won the hand of Princess Glauce. According to Hellenic [Greek] law, a man could enter into a marriage without a divorce from a previous wife. In Jason's case, he was especially free to act because his earlier marriage to Medea had been contracted with only barbarian oaths. He has already moved into the royal palace, while Medea and her children and some of her servants remain in the temporary refugee quarters.

THE ORDER OF BANISHMENT

Medea's old nurse comes out of the refugee lodge. She laments the brooding, gloomy despair into which her mistress has fallen. The children come back, romping with a ball, from a stroll they have been taking with their tutor. The tutor has heard the latest news, which is that Medea is to be told to leave.

Wild lamentation is now heard from within the shelter. It grows into a piercing song of Medea's resentment and denunciation. Her wailing has startled and stirred up the women of the neighborhood. In sympathy with her, they hasten to the scene. Their fellow feeling for Medea welds them into solidarity with her in her misfortune, in spite of her being an alien barbarian. The fate of women is the same everywhere.

Now Medea emerges from the lodge. A blonde woman, she is clothed in the Hellenic style. There is nothing to mark her as the wild sorceress, nothing to indicate her infamous reputation. She conceals the desperation of her state, now that she appears in public. She speaks to the women calmly and reasonably. Knowing now what threatens her, she is intelligent enough to listen quietly to King Creon, who arrives, accompanied by his bodyguard. He announces the order of deportation to her.

Medea confronts three men in the first half of the play. Each has more than one dramatic function in the action. Each stands as the representative of his sex against her as the representative of hers. Each of them speaks for his own generation. Jason is young. Creon is a white-bearded old man. Aegeus is in his forties.

Medea opposes each of them with the weapons and the consciousness of her attractive femininity. She is handsome and proud. She has magnetic charm.

By hypocritically throwing herself at Creon's knees, she succeeds in winning from him a concession of one day's delay in carrying out the order of banishment. She needs this time to carry out the program of vengeance she is planning, for she will not stand for being ridiculed by her enemies. Then Creon becomes angry at his own weakness in dealing with her. "I was not born to be a tyrant," he confesses. Finally he hurls his decree at her. She will be subjected to death by stoning if she fails to leave Corinth the very next day.

The scene demonstrates Medea's irresistible effect on men. This is due not to any of her magic arts, but only to the glamor of her womanhood. Euripides is clear about what he is doing. It is the destiny of women.

This woman, with her children, is being deserted by her husband. That was and is not unusual. It was regarded as perfectly ethical in the Hellas of that time. The wife had no opportunity to protest or to seek legal redress. Had she dared to do the same thing, she would have had to account for it.

Jason's treatment of Medea was considered acceptable by his society. The Hellenic women in the chorus realize it is futile to rebel against this treatment. Reason dictates they must reconcile themselves to male oppression. But Medea is not prepared to accept the male code so supinely. Her willfulness is due not to her barbarian inheritance but to her innate heroism. From their myths the Hellenes knew many such women who refused to reconcile themselves.

One of the women tells Medea that she is not the first woman to be so victimized. They advise her not to feel such bitterness over what cannot be changed. But she will not surrender submissively. She determines to use the power she herself possesses, that which has little to do with law and custom, and to apply her knowledge and audacity to what has happened to her. In the name of her sex, she challenges the lords of her world.

JASON EXPLAINS HIMSELF

Medea's plan for vengeance has now been perfected. Jason enters. There is not much more that can be said about him. This is the man with whom Medea was deeply in love, for whose sake she did so much that was frightful and criminal. He was her ideal, to whom she devoted herself entirely. His bearing is that of an aristocrat. Every gesture he makes shows his superior breeding. He is every inch the gentleman, the pattern every young man in Hellas would wish to emulate.

Jason is not conscious of having acted shamefully to Medea. He has merely done what any man in his place would do. Through his marriage to Princess Glauce he is now prince consort and heir to the throne of Corinth. What is useful is good. This is what he tries to explain to Medea. He wanted to get out of this hovel on the outskirts of the city. He wanted to achieve a better life for himself and bring up his children as their lineage entitles them to be raised. It would eventually benefit their mother as well. That is all there is to it.

And all this would have gone smoothly if only Medea had acted sensibly. But she has gone about shrieking for justice and uttering threats against the royal family. Can one blame them if they resent such talk and wish her out of the country? Unfortunately, their animosity has spread to the children. Princess Glauce has insisted that Medea and her children be sent away. But Medea unfortunately thinks only about having Jason in bed with her. It is this way of thinking that a cultivated gentleman despises to the uttermost. He does not permit himself to be controlled by his passions. He keeps his head clear and bears himself irreproachably. It is not his way to allow his feelings free play as Medea does. Then, as now, it is easy to foresee his conclusion: Medea must understand that the necessary is not sordid.

What does Jason now want? To show her how big-hearted he is, he has hurried to offer her money and letters of introduction to her place of exile. He appears after hearing that Creon had granted her one more day in Corinth. Why not before? He admits that he loves his children. It will pain him to part with them, but Medea alone is to blame for that.

She persuades him to make a last effort to obtain permission for the children to live in the palace at Corinth. It would take only a little good will from the others to accomplish that much. Jason, believing he knows how to manipulate the royal family, agrees to arrange it. But why did he not try to do that before? Medea rejects his money and his letters. He is indignant and calls on the gods to witness that he has offered her everything that could be expected of him. So he leaves, as Medea calls after him to go to his wench.

THE KING OF ATHENS OFFERS REFUGE

Aegeus, king of Athens, happens to be passing by. . . . Aegeus is on his way back from Delphi, where he went to consult Apollo about his childlessness. He is on his way to Troezen, a city on the northwest coast of the Peloponnesus well known to Athenians. Troezen is the birthplace of Theseus, the national hero of Athens. Aegeus, the third man in this drama, will be the progenitor of Theseus, though at this point his supposed impotence has not yet been cured. Vigorous, jovial, impressive, he is in the prime of life. Medea and Jason are old acquaintances of his. He greets Medea warmly when he sees her and stops his royal train. It is a joyful meeting for him.

Medea has just been giving vent to her sorrows. She seizes the opportunity to talk. Aegeus has turned up as if she had sent for him. His appearance would also explain her later residence in Athens, according to the tradition. He asks why she is grieving. When Medea confides that Jason has deserted her, he responds with indignation. To her complaint that Jason cannot be faithful, he tells her to let him go. So far, so good. But now she exposes Jason's perfidy. Who is her successor? The crown princess of Corinth. Taken aback, Aegeus now understands why she is so unhappy.

But, Medea tells him, that is not the worst of it. She has been banished from Corinth. Aegeus is stern that Jason is permitting that. Now, however, he restrains his indignation. There is a disconcerting silence, after which Aegeus's switch becomes apparent. Nothing remains of his first spontaneous reaction of shock. Aegeus is fearful of being involved in complications. Athens, Corinth—this could become a political issue.

Medea grasps the initiative. For the second time she shows her magic power. For the second time she drops to her knees before a man. She grasps his hand, begging him to take her into his home. But it is not as simple as all that. She knows what men are like. She must offer something in exchange. She promises that the gods will reward him for his generosity. But what is more to the point, she will give him drugs that will enable him to beget children. A long silence. Aegeus makes no effort to raise Medea from her knees. He has to make a political decision. Eventually, he arrives at a crafty solution.

He will guarantee Medea asylum. But he cannot take her with him out of Corinth. She must first leave Corinth on her own and then seek refuge in Athens. There she may live in safety. He will hand her over to no one.

But Medea has in mind the enormity of the deeds she intends to perform before leaving Corinth. What would Aegeus do if he were requested by Corinth to hand her over? She rises. Seizing upon his offer, she asks him to take a vow. It is a great moment for her in the play. With impressive power she prescribes the oath he must swear. He repeats it obediently, following her dictation. She coerces him into agreeing that should he violate his vow he will submit to the punishment that is imposed on one guilty of sacrilege. With this he departs. No word of farewell.

Another man. Like all the rest. This one will be the father of democracy. He thinks only of his own advantage. She calls good wishes after him.

MEDEA'S HIDEOUS CRIME

The second half of the play whips past, rushed along because the action, according to the rules of classical tragedy, must be completed within the span of one day. Carried along by emotional excitement, the action builds up toward the climax, which is the murder of the children. Why is this necessary? Why must the children die? Medea, obsessed by her plan of vengeance, shows a kind of cold frenzy coupled with the utmost sagacity [wisdom].

In a long monologue, Medea discloses the steps of her scheme. She will ask Jason to return. Pretending to be submissive, she will ask his pardon. She will pretend to be reconciled. She will play upon his trust to make him her instrument, getting him to take gifts from her children to the palace.

One gift will be a frock of wondrous beauty, impregnated with a fiery poison. The princess will put it on. The poison will begin its work only when the children are on the way home to their mother. Then it will be mortal. The princess will feel her whole body is being eaten alive. Whoever attempts to tear the dress off her body will himself be overcome by the corroding acid. This will destroy the princess's father as well.

It is clear to Medea what will happen after the perpetration of this hideous crime. Neither she nor the children will be permitted to escape. If she wants to prevent her enemies from taking revenge on the children, she will have to kill them herself.

The scheme works out according to her plan. At first Jason refuses to take the gifts, but, when assured they are for his young bride, agrees. The children carry the small parcels with the gifts in them. Completely absorbed in carrying out her design, Medea approaches the moment that obsesses her, her moment of triumph over her enemies. In this way she arrives at the scene that will become the peak of high dramatic art for all time, her monologue before the murder of her children.

Only when things have progressed to this point does her obsession break. Her children return from the palace. Suddenly, the maternal instinct within her wells up. With the aid of the gods she has caught herself in her own net.

The death of her children was the part of her plan of vengeance that was meant to pierce Jason to the heart. Now she feels her own heart fatally pierced. Conflict begins to tear her apart. How can she take life away from the children who look at her with trusting eyes? Yet, how can she let her jeering enemies injure her without reprisal? She draws her children close to her and embraces them. Knowing what she is going to do, she cannot look at them any longer if she is to maintain her revengeful anger. The children are led into the house. At first Medea feels that she cannot do this foul deed.

But her moments of vacillation grow shorter and shorter. At last she suppresses her tender feelings. Her children are not to live their lives as targets of ridicule. Now she speaks lines that have lived through the years: the daemonic instinct that is the source of all mental ills, the need that must be satisfied above emotions, directs her clearly.

ESCAPE IN A FLYING CHARIOT

A long silent scene follows. Medea crouches on the steps like a statue. The chorus sings a deeply pensive passage. . . .

When Medea speaks once more, she mounts a raised platform. From this she will be the first to see the messenger coming with the news of the outcome of her action. She stands there for a period, staring into the distance. She is waiting to hear some outcry, some demonstration, some message for her, some tidings. Whatever the news will be, she will have time to dash into the house, make the door fast inside, and perform the last act of her dreadful plot.

Euripides prescribed the composition of a highly expressive musical accompaniment to heighten and intensify the moments of the actual murder scene. Desperate cries are heard from within. The women outside beat a drum-fire pounding against the locked entrance door and shout imprecations against the murderer. Finally, Jason appears, utterly distraught, in violent haste to save the children from royal vengeance, with his sword in hand to cut their mother down. This, then, is the ending.

The conclusion is in the form of a miracle. Above the roof of the house a flying chariot swung ex machina in the same gondola device generally used to produce the deus ex machina. The wings are those of the dragons who seem to be moving it.

At its first production this glittering stage effect must have been a most impressive success, because it was copied innumerable times. The audience saw the bodies of the dead children hanging through the lattice work of the cart. Medea wears a magnificent oriental robe, a diadem [crown] sparkles in her blonde hair. Everything glows in the rays of the sun. Jason is left groaning as he recoils from the door he has broken open. From on high, Medea declaims her triumphant verses. Her enemies can ridicule her no longer. She will bury her children up on the promontory, the Acrocorinth, where Hera has her temple. Then she will fly to sanctuary in Athens.

The Play Is Structured Around Scenes of Confrontation

John Ferguson

This informative, perceptive, and well-written essay by John Ferguson, former director of studies at England's Open University, analyzes the structure of Euripides' *Medea*. As Ferguson explains, the three key scenes are those between Medea and Jason, which frame the piece. The other scenes, which bridge these three, give essential information, develop the characters, build suspense, and/or provide emotional relief. The scene between Medea and Aegeus, king of Athens, says Ferguson, does all four of these things.

The structure of the play is built around the three scenes of confrontation between Jason and Medea. The first follows the choral ode, and it is superlative. It is characteristic of Euripides that by Medea's bitter outburst at the end of the previous scene he has caused our sympathy to recede from her. Now we see Jason, cold, reasonable, not wanting to be thought a cad. "Even if you do hate me, I could never think badly of you" (463), he says—to the woman who loves him and whom he has taken! . . . Medea in contrast shows a passionate hatred that would revert to love at one sign from him. "I saved your life," she hisses in words where every other letter is an *s*. A little earlier the nurse described her as made wild like a bull (188). Now she reminds him that she helped him yoke the fire-breathing bulls (478). She is now the bull, and he will not have her help to establish control. The themes of promise breaking (492, 511) and Greek arrogance (509) throb through her outburst. And before her passion Jason reefs his sail and remains calm, reasonable and utterly despicable, ending with the brutal words that the world would be better without woman—a pleasant promise for his prospective bride. Jason offers Medea everything except the thing for which she yearns. She asks for nothing except the thing he will not give. "Love," wrote [noted scholar Gilbert] Murray perceptively, "to her is the whole world, to him it is a stale memory." The scene ends in defiance.

The chorus sings, again briefly, again eloquently, again relevantly. There is no greater joy than love in moderation. In excess it destroys reputation and moral principle. The women pray for that saving wisdom which is . . . moderation or self-control; but they know that these things are beyond human power. Euripides has many great songs to love. Some are more powerful, none is more delicate. Then they pass from a theme that reflects the previous scene to one that anticipates the next. They deplore the thought of exile. No city, no friend pitied Medea in her suffering. Enter Aegeus.

THE BRIGHTNESS OF ATHENS, THE DARKNESS OF CORINTH

The scene that follows was criticized by Aristotle as irrelevant, a clumsy device to give Medea a refuge, and [classical scholar Gilbert] Norwood talks about the utter futility of the scene. This is a misunderstanding. No one would worry if Medea escaped in the sun chariot without Athens as a destination, though once Euripides has conceived the scene he uses it pivotally, leading up to it and away from it. The function of the scene is first to provide relief. It is the one tranquil scene in the play, and in its historical context, to an Athenian audience, it is something more. It is the lull before the storm. It contrasts the brightness of Athens with the darkness of Corinth. Second, it shows us another Medea, a princess in her own right, courteous, genuinely—need we doubt it?—concerned about the troubles of others. Third, the scene is pivotal to the theme of childlessness. It is here that as Medea promises to turn Aegeus from childlessness to the possession of children, she resolves to turn Jason from the possession of children to childlessness. It is important at the same time to see the reverse side of this; there is an important emotional counterweight to her killing of the children in her gift of children to Aegeus. Fourth, Aegeus is beautifully delineated. He is not to be thought of as old; after all [the great Athenian hero] Theseus is to be his son, and is grown to manhood when he dies. He is full of his own troubles and thinks that everyone else wants to know about them. It is some time before he realizes that anything is wrong with Medea. Then he is sympathetic, though he needs a great deal of prodding before he offers help. Fifth, Euripides is able to introduce the traditional riddling phallic response from Delphi (679). Oral societies love riddles, especially with a sexual slant—witness West Africa today—and ancient Greece was no exception. Sixth, in this pivotal scene, Medea kneels for the second time to a man (710), and for the second time she has her way. Finally, the theme of the promise returns with strength in the mighty oath that Medea exacts from Aegeus and that holds the stage for no less than twenty-five lines (731). After he has gone, Medea invokes Zeus, who is among other things god of oaths, justice as daughter of Zeus, and the light of the Sun. She has found a harbor (769). She reveals her plan to the chorus, to speak softly to Jason, the use of the children as a trap, to send by them a poisoned dress to the girl, and then to kill them. She ends with the words:

> Let no one imagine I am poor, weak
> and peaceable. The opposite is true.
> I am cruel to my enemies and generous to my friends.
> That's the way to a life of glory. (807)

The chorus tries ineffectually to dissuade her, but she sends for Jason. It is noteworthy that Euripides, who is evidently here inventing his plot, at this stage of his career feels constrained to reveal it in advance, in accordance with the normal convention that the basic plot is known.

THE VIPER BENEATH THE STONE

The choral ode that follows is of great beauty. It is a hymn in praise of Athens. But here too the first two stanzas look back to the scene with Aegeus, the next two forward to the murder of the children. As they try to persuade themselves that she will not bring herself to the act, Jason appears, and we see her justification. This is the second confrontation. Medea is hypocritically subservient, Jason complacently compliant; even in his egotism we pity his blindness.

We may note five points. First, when we hear her hypocritical words the way has been prepared by the scene with Creon. There we thought at first the emotion sincere; when Creon went out she revealed a savage exultation. Here from the first we discern the viper beneath the stone. Second, she tells the children to take their father's right hand (899). This is a deliberate echo of some words she has earlier spoken to

Jason: "Ah, my hand, which you so often grasped" (496). As Jason deceived her, she deceives him. Action and reaction are equal and opposite. Third, in the middle of the scene Medea bursts into tears for the children. In the ancient world some insensitive critics blamed Euripides for inconsistency here. It is of course magnificent. Medea does love the children; how could she not? But her love and hatred for Jason is greater than her mother love. Euripides knows the human heart better than these ancient professors. Fourth, Medea tells Jason to command his wife (His wife! Did be ever command Medea?) to plead with her father to annul the children's banishment. The next two lines should both be given to Jason. He replies:

> Yes, and I reckon they will persuade her—
> if she's like the rest of women. (944)

The rest of women!—with Medea there, in Jason's blinkered eyes so pliable and easy. Finally, the last words to the children as she sends them off with poisoned gifts are terrible:

> Go quickly. Be successful. Bring
> your mother the good news she longs to hear. (974)

There follows a choral song of utter hopelessness, and the tutor and children are back. The tutor brings what he believes to be good news of the acceptance of the gifts and the reprieve of the children, and wrings a cry of momentary despair from Medea. The tutor thinks that it is the prospect of separation that disturbs her, and offers patronizing consolation in words of bitter irony to her:

> TUTOR: Cheer up! Your children will bring you home.
> MEDEA: First I have others to bring home. (1015)

He goes, and what follows is possibly the finest speech in all Greek tragedy, as all Medea's mother love pours out to the children, only to be blotted out by her fury. She says goodbye as if she were leaving them, but we grimly know that they will leave her. Twice she stands on the verge of giving up her scheme. Once it is the thought of her enemies' mockery that moves her, once the realization that the other murder is committed and things cannot be the same. In all we see a true woman. It is a superb piece of artistry, backed by profound understanding of the human will.

A FURTHER PERIOD OF SUSPENSE

The killing of the children is not yet. Euripides knows his Medea too well; she could not act until she knew that the rest of her revenge had succeeded. Euripides also knows his theater too well; a further period of suspense gives added power, and the murder of the children must come after the narrative of the girl's death, as the culminating horror. A choral chant follows. We wonder what more Euripides can say, yet he finds something fresh and appropriate—a processional-type song . . . that starts from the praise of women, and whose central theme is the blessing of not having children. Children are a delight, but they are also a worry; they need looking after, and may turn out badly or die. To our sophisticated society this is almost a cynical commonplace. To an ancient Greek, as to a modern African audience, the death of a son was deeply held, but the suggestion that it is better to be childless would appear a scandalous paradox.

The death of the children is the crowning agony. Enter the messenger. It is hard not to use superlatives in writing of *Medea*, and the messenger's speech is among the finest of its kind. It is a brilliantly vivid narrative. We see the joy of the servants in the reconciliation. The messenger speaks of "the mistress whom we now honor instead of you" (1144)—it has happened so swiftly that he does not realize that she is dead. We see her with eyes only for Jason, jealous of Medea's children, excited over the fine clothes—she was, after all, only a teenager. Then follows the dreadful account of the death agonies of the girl and her father—it is Creon not Jason who goes to the rescue—clinical in its observation, but with a bitterly excited identification with the scene. Where is the traditional reticence of Greek art? Nowhere. Euripides is not interested. The grandeur of Medea's passion brings destruction on a colossal scale. To minimize this would be to minimize his theme. He plays nothing down. He does not now seek our sympathy for Medea's suffering, only our fear at the power of her love. He speaks to each man in the audience: "You unfaithful husbands, suppose this power, which is in your wife, for that she like Medea is a woman—suppose it flared out."

THE FINAL CONFRONTATION

The messenger goes, and the chorus comments that the divine power is fitting together a weight of disaster for Jason, as he deserves. Medea speaks directly. She is resolved to kill the children and escape. Still she half wavers, still she is their mother. Then she goes in. We hear the great bolts clang shut. The chorus, helpless, raise a prayer to Earth and the

Sun to intervene, in a splendid tableau; then in an equally fine tableau turn their backs to the audience and sing to Medea in the house, appealing to her better nature, her mother love. Their song is cut off by a scream. What can they do? Another scream. And then they rush from the orchestra onto the stage and beat with bare hands at the barred door. So far from the chorus being, as some critics have alleged, detached and inactive, they are involved and active, powerfully, dramatically, unconventionally, boldly active. The screams continue—and then stop. It is over. Then and only then does the flute start again; with somber steps they return to the orchestra and sing a sad song about children killed in legend. The death of the children is transfigured by being seen as a part of timeless sorrow. To understand this is to understand the soul of Greek tragedy; to fail to understand it is to leave empty formalism and dead convention.

Jason rushes in with an armed guard and learns from the chorus of the children's death. He sends his men to burst open the doors. We are expecting the moving platform with the bodies [the "tableau-machine," a common stage device in Greek tragedy]. Suddenly at the top of the building there is Medea in a great golden-winged chariot; the bodies of the children are with her. It is a magnificent moment. . . . So we have the final confrontation. Jason is a pricked balloon, a jelly of self-pity. His vaunted self-control broken, he curses Medea as Medea has cursed him, but the curses are empty words. He is incapable of action. Argo [the ship on which he sailed heroically to recover the Golden Fleece] was his one action, as he nostalgically recalls, and that is past. In the present he can do nothing and is nothing. Medea, triumphant, exultant, has complete victory. In the first confrontation Jason has power, Medea apparently only words, and the end is defiance. In the second, there is apparent reconciliation. Jason seems to have control of the action, but we know that Medea has control in fact. In the third, Jason has only words, Medea power, and the end is defiance.

Euripides Enriches the Text with a Reference to Another Child Killer

Rick M. Newton

The ancient Greek dramatists often made allusions to characters and situations in other myths that were similar to those featured in their own plays. Their audiences naturally understood these literary references because they were familiar with these myths, just as almost all Christians today are familiar with biblical stories such as Adam and Eve, Noah's Ark, and the parting of the Red Sea. Here, Kent State University scholar Rick M. Newton examines one such mythological reference employed by Euripides at the climax of *Medea*, when the lead character is off-stage killing her children and the Chorus stands on stage helpless and in despair. The myth in question is that of Ino, originally the daughter of Cadmus, king of Thebes, and a nursemaid to the infant god Dionysus. In the story, the goddess Hera, Zeus's wife, jealous of Zeus's affair with the child's mother, attempts to destroy the infant. In the process, Hera drives poor Ino mad and the young woman jumps into the sea, taking her own son, Melicertes, with her. Subsequently, to Hera's dismay, both Ino and Melicertes rise from the dead, having been miraculously transformed into minor sea-gods.

In the fifth stasimon [choral song] of Euripides' *Medea*, the chorus of Corinthian women prays to the earth and sun to stop Medea from carrying out the plans to murder her children. After one strophe [movement] and antistrophe [countermovement], however, the cries of the boys are heard from within the house as Medea stabs them to death. The prayer has come too late. As the chorus sings the final antistrophe, they search for a precedent for such a horrendous deed: Ino, driven mad by Hera, laid a murderous hand on her own children and afterward leapt to her death in the sea. It is the aim of this paper to examine the significance and dramatic impact of Euripides' choice of Ino as a paradigm [model] for Medea.

PRECEDENTS FOR SHOCKING DEEDS

Tragic choruses frequently allude to *exempla* [similar examples from the past] when acts of violence occur, or are about to occur, in a play. These allusions, drawn from the remote realm of myth, provide poetic embellishment for the tragic *pathē* [dramatic suffering] currently taking place. The allusions also serve the important function of establishing in the minds of both chorus and audience precedents for the shocking deeds. Seen within the broader context thereby established, the *pathē* are mitigated in their severity. Indeed, one may even argue that the events being dramatized are, in a sense, predictable. For what has happened before is likely to happen again. The ultimate result of the evocation of precedents is to render the horrors less shocking. In Aeschylus's *The Libation Bearers* 585–651, for example, immediately after Orestes enlists the silent cooperation of the Libation Bearers in his plot against Clytemnestra, the chorus recites a catalogue of women notorious for treachery against relatives: Althaea killed her son, Scylla caused the death of her father Nisus, and the Lemnian wives slew their husbands in a mass murder. Just as these wicked women have paid the price for their foul deeds, so too now Orestes is planning to avenge the "old blood" (650) shed by Clytemnestra, another candidate for the list. The paradigms serve to convince the chorus and the audience that it is indeed proper for Orestes to seek revenge in the "blameless crime"... of matricide. A similar pattern can be discerned in Sophocles' *Antigone* 944–87. As Antigone is led to her rocky tomb, the Theban elders sing of other victims of punishment by confinement: Danae was pent in a chest, Lycurgus was imprisoned in a cave, and Cleopatra was raised in the cave of Boreas. Antigone's fate, therefore, is far from unique. The chorus points out that individuals of even greater stature than she have suffered so.... These remarks can hardly comfort the heroine, but they are doubtless welcome to the ears of Creon, the austere tyrant whom the citizens secretly fear but openly obey. The cowering chorus cites these paradigms to voice their approval of

Creon's measures and to imply that they would never court disaster by challenging his authority. . . .

INO AND MEDEA BOTH DEIFIED?

Examined in the light of these passages, the reference to Ino in the *Medea* stands out as unusual. As in the other dramas discussed, here too the chorus is closely involved with the action of the play. Convinced that Medea is justified in seeking revenge against her enemies, the Corinthian women have sworn

---

WOMEN FILLED WITH PASSION AND PAIN

This excerpt from Philip Vellacott's translation of Medea *contains the playwright's complete reference to the Ino myth.*

A child's scream is heard from inside the house.
CHORUS: Do you hear? The children are calling for help.
   O cursed, miserable woman!
CHILDREN'S VOICES: Help, help! Mother, let me go!
   Mother, don't kill us!
CHORUS: Shall we go in?
   I am sure we ought to save the children's lives.
CHILDREN'S VOICES: Help, help, for the gods' sake! She is
   killing us!
   We can't escape from her sword!
CHORUS: O miserable mother, to destroy your own increase,
Murder the babes of your body!
Stone and iron you are, as you resolved to be.

   There was but on in time past,
   One woman that I have heard of,
   Raised hand against her own children.
   It was Ino, sent out of her mind by a god,
   When Hera, the wife of Zeus,
   Drove her from her home to wander over the world.
   In her misery she plunged into the sea
   Being defiled by the murder of her children;
   From the steep cliff's edge she stretched out her foot,
   And so ended,
   Joined in death with her two sons.

   What can be strange or terrible after this?
   O bed of women, full of passion and pain,
   What wickedness, what sorrow you have caused on the
      earth!

Euripides, *Medea*, in Philip Vellacott, trans., *Euripides: Medea and Other Plays.*
New York: Penguin Books, 1963, pp. 56–57.

---

their silence if Medea should discover "any means or contrivance" (260) to retaliate against Jason, Creusa, and Creon. "I will do as you wish," promises the Coryphaeus [chorusleader]. "For you will punish your husband justly". . . . But when, in the fifth stasimon, this revenge manifests itself unexpectedly in infanticide, the silent accomplices find themselves at a loss: speaking separately . . . they deliberate, "Shall I enter the house to save the children?" (1275–76). Searching for precedents which will mollify their horror and justify their involvement, they recall "one and only one woman from the past". . . . The single choice of Ino strikes the audience as abrupt, for in parallel situations in other plays the chorus cites two or three paradigms in succession. The suggestion therefore presents itself that the poet is suppressing other examples. For Euripides could easily have supplemented the ode with allusions to other women guilty of filicide. . . . We may wonder, then, why the poet selected the Ino myth and excluded other *exempla,* some of which may have been more apposite.

The Ino myth contains elements which render it particularly harmonious with the events in the *Medea*. First, the tradition of Ino's deification . . . after her leap into the sea anticipates the final tableau, which presents Medea in the chariot of the Sun [which seems to give her god-like qualities]. . . . A second feature of the Ino myth which enhances the play is the poignant paradox that Ino, in attempting to save Melicertes from her husband Athamas, becomes herself her child's killer: when Athamas is driven mad by Hera, he shoots his son Learchus with an arrow; Ino, witnessing the scene, takes Melicertes in her arms and flees for safety, jumping with him into the sea. Medea's actions display the same paradox. For after she momentarily succumbs to pity for the boys and renounces her plans, she considers what will happen if she lets them live: "By the avenging spirits of Hades, it will never be that I leave my children to suffer insolence at the hands of my enemies" (1059–61). In killing her children, the distraught heroine believes that she is protecting them from her foes. Finally, Ino resembles Medea in that each of them has two sons. . . .

RECONSTRUCTING BOTH MYTHS

It is in the detail of the number of children slain by Ino, however, that the poet surprises us. For although variations exist within the story, one detail remains constant throughout the tradition: Athamas kills Learchus, and Ino kills Melicertes. But the Corinthian women clearly allude here to a version in which Ino commits the "ungodly murder of her offspring" and "perishes in dying with the two children." It is possible, of course, that they are referring to a version which, though now lost to us, the ancient audience would have recognized. But it is also possible that the poet is introducing a change in the myth. . . . The possibility of innovation becomes a probability when we consider the larger context of the allusion. For it is well known that the plot of the play revolves around a shocking change in the mythological tradition: Euripides is the first to present Medea as the deliberate murderess of her sons. Indeed, when she declares her real intentions in 792–93, the chorus reacts with shock and disbelief: "Will you dare . . . to kill your own flesh and blood?" "When you look at them . . . and they fall to supplicate you, you will not be able to do it". . . . But Medea plunges ahead, deaf to all attempts at dissuasion. At the very moment that she commits the foul deed, the poet does not, as we normally expect, cushion the shock with a catalogue of well-known mythological paradigms. Instead, he drives our sense of horror even deeper by likening the crime to Ino's murder of her two sons, an event which never occurred. Just as Euripides "demythologizes" the heroine of the play and constructs a new myth around her, so too here he presents in the passing reference to Ino a small-scale version of the same process. Simply stated, there are no genuine mythological examples to mitigate the horror of Medea's actions. For Ino offers no parallel. . . . The spectator is tempted to correct the chorus with the retort, "There is not one woman from the past who ever went to such extremes, not even Ino."

The Use of the *Deus ex Machina*

H.D.F. Kitto

One of the many stage devices invented by Greek playwrights in the fifth century B.C. was the *deus ex machina*, most often translated as "the god from the machine." The "machine" was a mechanical crane (the exact shape of which is unknown and likely varied) that flew actors and props above the acting area to create special dramatic effects. Sometimes the device was used to depict mythical heroes, for instance the courageous Bellerophon riding his winged horse, Pegasus. But most often the characters flown above were gods, who usually appeared in the end of a play to intervene in the action and bring the story to a satisfactory, logical, or fair conclusion. In *Medea*, it is the title character who utilizes the *deus*, in this case floating above the stage in a chariot drawn by dragons. As explained here by the late, great classical scholar H.D.F. Kitto, many critics, beginning with the Greek philosopher Aristotle, have decried Euripides' use of the device here; but Kitto convincingly shows how truly fitting, thematically logical, and dramatically satisfying it actually is.

As to the end of the play Aristotle's words are:

> In the characters as in the composition of the plot one must always aim at an inevitable or a probable order of events, so that it will be either inevitable or probable that such a person should say or do such a thing, and inevitable or probable that this thing should happen after that. It is obvious therefore that the ending too of the plot must arise naturally out of the plot itself, and not, as in the *Medea*, by external contrivance.

This is not an objection to the *Deus ex machina* as such, only to such employments of it as we have here. The *Philoctetes* [a play by Euripides' colleague, Sophocles] ends

Excerpted from H.D.F. Kitto, *Greek Tragedy*. Reprinted with permission from Taylor & Francis Books Ltd.

with a Deus, but the appearance of Heracles there is to some
extent a natural result of the action of the play; it has at least
been prepared for by the importance in the play of his magic
bows and arrows. In the *Medea*, there has been nothing of
this magic background; on the contrary, the background has
been at times painfully prosaic [matter-of-fact and straight-
forward]. We have had a scene of bitter domestic strife in a
setting of ordinary social life—children, nurses, curious
neighbours, old men gossiping around the spring. Medea may
be the granddaughter of Helios [god of the sun], but for all that
we are dealing with ordinary life and never feel that the gods
are within call. Medea quite rationally, and to the detriment of
the play, provides herself with a refuge; why then is an un-
natural means of escape provided for her at the end?

RESCUED BY THE SUN

It is of course some answer to say that Medea is a barbarian
princess and a magician; she is descended from Helios, and
she is in possession of certain mysterious powers, or more
strictly poisons, which ordinary women know nothing
about. We are the less surprised therefore at her miraculous
escape. . . . This may be true, but at the most it is only a pal-
liation; it made Euripides' error possible.

But if we look carefully into the last scene we shall see
more than dramatic convenience in the chariot. Medea has
done things which appal even the chorus, those sympathetic
neighbours who had said, earlier in the play, 'Now is honour
coming to womankind.' Their prayer now is 'O Earth, O thou
blazing light of the Sun, look upon this accursed woman before she slays her own children. . . . O god-given light, stay
her hand, frustrate her . . .' (1251 ff.). In the same vein Jason
says, when he has learnt the worst, 'After doing this, of all
things most unholy, dost thou show thy face to the Sun and
the Earth?' (1327). Sun and Earth, the most elemental things
in the universe, have been outraged by these terrible crimes;
what will they do? how will they avenge their sullied purity?
What Earth will do we shall not be told, but we are told what
the Sun does: he sends a chariot to rescue the murderess.

Is this illogical? Could anything be finer, more imaginative? . . . In [another of Euripides' plays,] the *Hippolytus*, although reason must be our guide, the primitive things in the
universe—Aphrodite and Artemis there—are not reasonable. The servant of Hippolytus thinks what Jason and the

chorus [in *Medea*] think, that 'Gods should be wiser than men'. Perhaps so, but these gods are not. They exist; as well deny the weather as deny Aphrodite; but they are not reasonable and can make short work of us. Zeus, 'whoever he is', is another matter. There may be a *Noũs*, a Mind, in the universe; but there are other powers too, and these we may worship in vain. The magic chariot is a frightening glimpse of something that we . . . see in full force in [Euripides'] the *Bacchae*, the existence in the universe of forces that we can neither understand nor control—only participate in.

A NECESSARY CLIMAX

The end of the *Medea* does not come out of the logic of the action by the law of necessity and probability, but is contrived by Euripides, deliberately, as the final revelation of his thought. When we begin to see Medea not merely as the betrayed and vindictive wife but as the impersonation of one of the blind and irrational forces in human nature, we begin to find that catharsis for which we looked in vain in the messenger-speech. It is this transformation that finally explains the 'revolting' and deepens a dramatic story into tragedy. Had Euripides been content with a 'logical' ending, with the play remaining on the mundane, Corinthian level, the 'revolting' would indeed have needed justification. This makes demands on our tolerance which cannot be met if the only profit is the news that barbarian magicians who are passionate and are villainously treated do villainous things. There is in the *Medea* more than this, and to express that Euripides resorts to a manipulation of the plot, an artificial ending which, like Aegeus [king of Athens, who gives Medea refuge in his city after she commits her crimes], would have been ruinous to Sophocles. This imaginative and necessary climax is not the logical ending to the story of Medea the ill-used wife of Corinth, but it is the climax to Euripides' underlying tragic conception.

Ancient and Modern Criticisms of the Play

Peter D. Arnott

A better understanding of the structure of *Medea* and
the playwright's reasons for including certain characters and scenes is afforded by examining the criti-
cisms leveled against the play over the centuries. In
this well-informed essay, noted scholar and translator Peter D. Arnott considers the supposed faults
most often cited by critics. First, he discusses Euripides' inclusion of important characters of common
birth, such as servants and slaves; then he examines
the scene between Medea and Aegeus, king of
Athens, the scene in which Medea appears high
above the stage in the dragon chariot, and the principal quarrel scene between Medea and Jason. After
refuting the objections to these aspects of the play,
Arnott suggests that one possible valid criticism of
the play is Euripides' use of the chorus, a theatrical
convention the playwright may not have been completely comfortable with.

Euripides was notorious in his own time for his attempts to
bring the theatre down to earth, and to narrow the gap between drama and life. [The fifth-century B.C. comic play-
wright] Aristophanes . . . censures his fondness for introducing characters from the lowest walks of life, not before
deemed worthy of a place on the tragic stage. We see two of
these in *Medea*, the Nurse and the Tutor—more accurately,
a slave charged with the supervision of Jason's children—
whom Euripides brilliantly utilizes the gossip of the servants' hall to create atmosphere, and to arouse sympathy for
Medea before she appears. The Tutor is a professed cynic
[one who believes that all people are motivated by selfish-
ness], a man who can see through the pretensions of his

Excerpted from Peter D. Arnott, trans. and ed., *Three Greek Plays for the Theater.*
Reprinted with permission from Indiana University Press.

masters; the Nurse is garrulous [overly talkative] but kindly, genuinely fond of her mistress and the children, a simple soul caught up in events far above her head. In her we see a preliminary sketch for the far more formidable figure of Phaedra's old nurse in *Hippolytus.* . . .

GIVING THE AUDIENCE A LINK WITH THEIR PAST

Of the [other] objections raised against *Medea* by ancient and modern critics, three deserve to be considered in some detail.

a) *The Aegeus scene.* Critics from Aristotle onwards have objected that the appearance of Aegeus is too obviously contrived, to provide Medea with the refuge of which she has just spoken. If we are to assess the play in naturalistic terms, there is certainly some truth in this. But a naturalistic interpretation is the very thing we must beware of. Even in Euripides' hands, Greek tragedy is still a highly formal art, and a realistic representation of life is by no means the major consideration. The poet is concerned rather with form and structure, and the importance of this episode in the structure of the work has already been demonstrated. In addition, Aegeus' plight performs an important function in formulating Medea's final plan of revenge. Up to this point, she has thought only of killing her husband. The childlessness of Aegeus suggests the more terrible punishment of leaving Jason alive, but killing the children, and thereby depriving him of everything that makes life worth living.

Nor must we underestimate the interest of this scene for an Athenian audience. Here is an Athenian king arriving in the nick of time to rescue a heroine in distress. The Greek tragedians were never above playing on such patriotic feelings. Aegeus was an important figure in the legendary history of Athens and the father of Theseus, unifier of Attica, whom he was to beget soon after leaving Corinth. Thus the scene gives the audience a link with their own past.

Finally, the Aegeus scene prepares the way for the dragon chariot at the end. Aegeus emphasizes the difficulties of removing Medea from Corinth. Perhaps there is another inconsistency here. Euripides makes him speak almost as if he already foresaw the course Medea's actions would take. He insists, no less than three times, that he will not be responsible for taking her to Athens, but that she must make her own way there. Although Aegeus can know nothing of the plot—this is still a secret between Medea and the chorus—Euripides communicates to him something of her anxiety. The method of escape becomes all-important. It should be said that this inconsistency is not detrimental, but merely serves to give the scene a greater sense of urgency.

BEWARE APPLYING MODERN STANDARDS TO ANCIENT TRAGEDY

b) *The dragon chariot.* This has been condemned as a spectacular appendage, adding nothing to the play but serving merely to delight the eye. Euripides is certainly fond of such devices. He uses processions, stage spectacle and crowd scenes wherever there is opportunity. Audiences of the later fifth century were beginning to develop a taste for such displays, and the abandonment of the earlier simplicity and restraint for vivid and colorful effects becomes more and more apparent, not only in the theatre but in the visual arts generally. Euripides, a born showman, pandered to this taste, and *Medea* lends itself readily to such treatment. We may conjecture, from the evidence of vase paintings, that Euripides gave Medea an exotic oriental costume, and the dragon chariot in particular seems to have struck the audience's attention. Spectacle aside, however, . . . the chariot plays an essential part in the play's diptychal structure [i.e., one made up of two halves of roughly equal importance]. To complete the perfect balance of the two halves, Medea must have a means of escape, and there is no illogicality in permitting her to call upon the resources of her witchcraft.

c) *The quarrel scene.* It has been objected that the confrontation of a faithless husband by his deserted wife, a scene calling for the wildest outpourings of passion, is here treated in too sophistical and artificial a spirit. Jason and Medea address each other in formal speeches, the first two of exactly equal length, and make points for the prosecution and defense more in the manner of a law-court than a domestic quarrel. But here again we must beware of applying modern standards to ancient tragedy. The Greek love of argument and debate, and, particularly in Athens, of litigation, permeates literature and the theatre, and does not confine itself to the courts and the council-house. It cannot be over-stressed that we are dealing here with formal drama, and that the set speeches, incongruous in the modern, naturalistic theatre, would have been accepted without comment

by a Greek spectator. Nor must we forget the physical limitations by which the dramatist was bound. A modern playwright treating the same episode could allow many of Medea's reactions to go unspoken. The actress would signify her reception of Jason's defense by facial expression alone. This was denied to Euripides [because of the great distance between the actors and the spectators]. Every point that Medea wishes to make, she must make verbally; and it is this that has led to the mistaken charges of artificiality and wordiness, by no means apparent in performance.

THE CHORUS AWKWARD?

Medea is a brilliant intellectual achievement, both as myth-criticism and an attack upon conventional morality. Although an early work, it demonstrates Euripides' technique at its most typical, and a masterly sense of construction. Its main weakness is one apparent throughout all Euripides' work, the handling of the chorus. At this stage in the history of the Greek theatre, the chorus has lost its old importance. Euripides, attempting to create a new type of realistic tragedy within the old conventional framework, finds it more and more of an embarrassment, particularly in plays of intrigue such as this, where the constant presence of the chorus makes it necessary for Medea, unnaturally, to confide in them. Nevertheless, the songs on the infidelity of man and in praise of Athens are two of his major choral compositions, worthy of a place beside those of Sophocles.

Medea, however, owes its survival more to its theatrical than to its purely intellectual qualities. The plays of Euripides, too unorthodox to be popular in his lifetime, were eagerly revived after his death, when the controversy that initially surrounded them was forgotten, and were performed far more frequently than those of Aeschylus or Sophocles. For Euripides is a master of the art of the theatre; his power to create exciting scenes and powerful characters has kept him popular with actors and audiences alike. In our own time, leading actresses—Katina Paxinou, Judith Anderson, Eileen Herlie, Sybil Thorndike—have found in the character of Medea a fit vehicle for their own talents. *Medea* ranks not far below *Oedipus Rex* as one of the most popular Greek Plays in the modern repertory.

CHAPTER 2

Themes and Ideas Explored in the Play

Euripides Prophecies a World of Violence and Discord

Bernard Knox

Among the most obvious themes exploited in *Medea*
are violence, discord, and disharmony, as shown by
the title character's murderous rampages. In this in-
sightful tract, Bernard Knox, director emeritus of
Harvard's Center for Hellenic Studies in Washington,
D.C., and one of the great classical historians of the
twentieth century, points out that Euripides wrote
the play just as such a violent world was about to become reality in Greece. Produced in 431 B.C., on the
eve of the long and disastrous Peloponnesian War,
says Knox, *Medea* seems, in retrospect, to point to
Athens's immediate future. And this makes the playwright's work all the more meaningful and relevant,
for it makes him a prophet as well as a describer of
social discord and violence.

Euripides was a many-sided poet; even in the fraction of his
work that has come down to us—about one-fifth—we can
hear many different voices . . . the realist who brought the
myths down to the level of everyday life; the inventor of the
romantic adventure play; the lyric poet . . . the producer of
patriotic war plays—and also of plays that expose war's ug-
liness in dramatic images of unbearable intensity; above all,
the tragic poet who saw human life not as action but as suffering. . . .

   We have nineteen of his plays—almost three times as many
as the seven of his contemporary and competitor Sophocles,
and the seven of his predecessor Aeschylus. We know him
better than the other two and yet we find him more difficult
to understand, to accept, to love. He seems unable or perhaps unwilling to resolve the discords his plays inflict on

Excerpted from Bernard Knox, *Backing into the Future: The Classical Tradition and Its
Renewal.* Reprinted with permission from W. W. Norton & Company.

our ears; even his masterpieces leave us full of disturbing questions. If he were not so great a dramatist we would suspect him of lack of direction, of faulty construction, of exploitation of dramatic effect without regard to structure, of rhetoric [speech-making] without regard for character; in fact many critics have tried him and found him guilty on some or all of these charges. But a man who could conjure up out of iambic lines and a mask such awesomely living figures as Medea, Phaedra, and Pentheus, who could round off the action of a play with final scenes like those of the *Trojan Women* or the *Hippolytus*, clearly knew his business as a dramatist. He must have intended to produce this unsettling effect, which disturbed his contemporaries as it disturbs us: to leave us with a sense of uncertainty, painfully conscious now, if not before, of the treacherous instability of the world in which we live, its utter unpredictability, its intractability. It might be said of him what the Corinthians in [the writings of the fifth-century B.C. Greek historian] Thucydides say of the Athenians, that he was born never to live in peace himself and to prevent the rest of mankind from doing so.

"THE SPRING HAS GONE OUT OF THE YEAR"

Nearly all the plays we have were written in the last twenty-five years of his life, the years of the Peloponnesian War. One of the most famous, and shocking, of them, the *Medea*, was first produced at the very start of that disastrous war, in the early spring (end of March—beginning of April) in the year 431 B.C. This was the spring festival of the god Dionysus, and the Athenians looked forward to it eagerly, for it marked the end of winter.

It had been a tense winter. Thucydides, who watched carefully the events of those months, intent, as he tells us, on writing the history of the war that was in the making, describes the atmosphere of that spring of 431 B.C. "Although war was imminent, the contending powers maintained diplomatic relations and exchanged representatives, but without confidence. For the preceding events were in fact a renunciation of the thirty years' peace treaty and anything now might provoke open hostilities" (I.146). We know this atmosphere very well; we lived in it from the end of World War II to the breakup of the Soviet Union—the Cold War, we called it. It did not, mercifully, turn into a hot one, a full-scale general conflict. In Greece it did, and the spark that set off the explosion was, as usual, an insignificant episode in it-self—the Theban attack on the small city of Plataea on a rainy night in March 431 B.C., the month and the year in which the *Medea* was produced.

This spring was the last spring of peace, of the Golden Age of Athens, the Periclean age, that period of enormous cre-ative activity in every field of endeavor, political, scientific, intellectual, artistic. This was the last spring: two years later Pericles, speaking of those who died in the opening battles, was to say, "the spring has gone out of the year."

In the *Medea* the chorus sings the praises of that Athens of the great, the Golden Age. "The Athenians . . . rich and happy from of old, sons of blessed divinities, inhabitants of a land which is holy, and undamaged by enemies; their diet is wis-dom, which brings them honor; they walk luxuriously through air which is brilliantly clear, a land where once, the story goes, the nine Muses were born to golden-haired Har-mony" (824–32). This description of an ideal Athens, set in a play in which a husband cynically betrays a wife and a mother murders her children, was sung in the theater of Dionysus at the very moment when what it described was about to disappear forever. "Rich and happy"—the wealth of Athens stored as golden plates on the . . . statue of Athena in the Parthenon was to be poured down the sink of nearly thirty years of war; the happiness, the Periclean sense of mastery of the environment, of control and balance, of un-limited horizons—all this was to go up in smoke, the smoke of the burning farmhouses and orchards in the Attic coun-tryside. The "land undamaged by enemies" was to feel the ax of the Spartan invader chopping down the olive trees. And wisdom was to go too—that sense of proportion, that bold initiative which yet recognized proper limits, the modera-tion of real understanding—all this was to die and fester in the plague that swept through the besieged, crowded city. The "brilliantly clear air" was to be clouded not only with the smoke from burning trees and houses but also with pas-sionate hatred, anger, greed, partisan accusation, ambitious demagoguery—"golden-haired Harmony" was to be re-placed by serpent-haired Discord.

A Prophet Is a Dangerous Thing to Be

And this is what the *Medea*, the *Hippolytus*, and Euripidean tragedy in general are about. It is a vision of the future. In it we can see at work the poet as prophet, as seer: *vates* the Romans called him, a word that means both poet and prophet.

The prophet is not a familiar figure in our modern civilization, but ancient Greece had many prophets human and divine who foretold the future, Apollo at Delphi the greatest among them. In the museum at Olympia one can see, among the figures on the pediment [of the remains of the Temple of Zeus] . . . the figure of the prophet—a bearded old man whose tense and tragic face shows that at this very moment he foresees all that is to come from that fatal charioteering: the children eaten by their father, the husband slaughtered by his wife, the mother cut down by her son. . . .

The poet as prophet lives not in the past, as most of us live—our attack on reality made with weapons that are already out of date—nor, as others live, in dreams of the future which turn away from the world as it is, but in the present, really in the present, seeing the present.

And this is what another poet-prophet, Arthur Rimbaud, meant when he said, *"Il faut être absolument moderne"*—one must be absolutely modern. This is what Euripides was, as he still is: absolutely modern.

But it is a dangerous thing to be. Rimbaud gave up poetry, left France to become an unsuccessful gun-runner in Abyssinia, and died of gangrene in a hospital in Marseilles, unknown, unrecognized. Euripides left his beloved Athens and went to spend his last years in the half-savage kingdom of Macedonia, where he died. The trouble with being absolutely modern is that you are ahead of all your contemporaries. You are, in fact, like all prophets, rejected and scorned by the present, to be acclaimed and understood by the future. It is the story of the Trojan princess Cassandra again: the divine gift of true prophecy and the condition that the prophet will not be believed. The prophet is rejected. With Euripides, in fact, begins the tradition of the poet not only as prophet but also as outcast and rejected. His career is a modern career. Unsuccessful throughout his life (he rarely won first prize and was the constant target of the comic poets), he became after his death the most widely read and most frequently performed Greek dramatist, eclipsing, and on the stage at any rate almost entirely extinguishing, the fame of his competitors. Euripides was understood not by his own generation but by the next and the generations that came after. . . .

ORDER AND FREEDOM A FADING MEMORY

The tragic world he created in the *Medea* . . . is an image of the world in which he lived, but few recognized the accuracy of that image. It shocked his contemporaries because they had not come to realize the nature of the world they lived in; still less could they imagine what sort of a world their sons and their sons' sons were to live in. One can forgive their dismay. The world Euripides created in the theater of Dionysus is one of disruption, violence, subversion, uncertainty, discord. . . .

The democratic regime established in Athens at the close of the sixth century had emerged triumphant from its trial by fire and sword, the Persian invasions of 490 and 480–79; the next half century saw the system consolidated at home on an increasingly egalitarian base and supported by the tribute from an Aegean empire which made Athens the dominant power in Greece. These were the years of confidence, of an outburst of energy, political, military, intellectual, and artistic, which astonished the world. There seemed to be no limits to what Athens—and Athenians—could achieve. It was in these years that Aeschylus produced his final masterpiece, the *Oresteia*, and Sophocles moved into his place to succeed him as the foremost poet in the theater of Dionysus. They spoke, through their actors and chorus, to a citizen body which, for all its diversity of income, status, and opinion, was fundamentally united on essentials; it was not until a long war had taken its toll . . . that the democratic regime was overthrown in 411 B.C. It was soon restored, but Athens was never the same again; the ideal city of the Periclean funeral speech, a vision of creative order, tolerance, and freedom, was now a fading memory.

And Euripides is the poet of the crackup: the *Medea* . . . [is a vision] of a divided city, a disordered universe, the nightmare in which the dream of the Athenian century was to end. Small wonder that Euripides was rejected by the majority, passionately admired by a few, but liked by no one. No nation, no society, welcomes the prophet of its own disintegration.

Misogyny in *Medea*

Eva Cantarella

Many historians have suggested that misogyny, a hatred and/or mistrust of women, lurked beneath the
surface of ancient Athenian society. They base this
view on the fact that women in Athens in Greece's
Classic Age (fifth and fourth centuries B.C.) led
largely restricted lives and had no political rights, as
men had. The theme of misogyny also occurs in
many of Euripides' plays, including *Medea.* This essay by Eva Cantarella, of Italy's University of Parma,
examines some of the lines from the play that express the social and moral denigration of women.
The question is whether the playwright meant to per-
petuate or to question and challenge women's second-class status in these lines. In Cantarella's opinion, it was more the former than the latter. (Scholars
remain more or less evenly divided on the issue.)

The literature of the classical period, which begins with the
tragedies of Aeschylus, gave its public important female
characters, images of women of strong character and proud
temperament capable of heroic and terrible deeds, women
like Antigone and Medea. But the tragedians' attitude toward
their heroines and toward the female sex in general has
been and continues to be the subject of debate.

THE OLD MISOGYNY

For some Hellenists, tragedy, and for that matter all the rest
of classical literature, reflects a profound disparagement of
women mixed with an invincible fear of their negative
power. For others (who believe that women enjoyed an ele-
vated social position), such characters as Aeschylus'
Clytemnestra or Sophocles' Antigone and Deianeira demon-
strate the Greeks' admiration for the female sex. Still others
(some of them women) maintain that we should make a

sharp distinction between Aeschylus and Sophocles on the one hand, and Euripides on the other. The infamous acts of many Euripidean heroines, says [the distinguished historian] S.B. Pomeroy (who notes in partial support of her position that British suffragists used to recite excerpts from Euripides), reveal the poet's desire to question the moral tradition and to denounce the difficult condition of women in his city.

The problem is far from simple. The complexity of the religious, ethical, and political significance of tragedy, together with the depth of the psychological analysis of the characters (expressions of the contradictions and drama of the human condition), makes it quite easy to fall into excessive simplification and too-rigid schematization. But, in my opinion, it is difficult to ignore the old misogyny and the equally old idea of the necessary subjugation of women in tragedy. Let us look at the women characters who have been called feminist. . . .

The tragedian whose work, albeit not without contradictions, seems best to express Greek misogyny is Euripides. Indisputably aware of the cultural ferments which, in the Athens of his time, questioned the subordination of women (and because of this considered by some to be the spokesman of the women's rebellion), Euripides confirms with utter certainty the old commonplace of the woman as "scourge, infamous race, unspeakable misfortune" for whoever cannot manage to escape her evil influence. He expresses this with uncommon virulence in the famous invective of Hippolytus:

> O Zeus, why have you settled women in the light of day, to be an evil counterfeit coin among men? For if you wanted to sow the seed of the human race, you needn't have provided it from *women,* but men could have deposited a sum of bronze or silver or gold in your temples to buy the seed of children for a certain price, each man for the amount appropriate to his estate, and men could live in free houses without women. . . . It is clear that women are a great evil for this reason: the father who begot and raised her pays a dowry to settle her elsewhere in order to relieve himself of trouble. The man who takes the destructive creature home happily puts out adornment for his most evil idol and completely spends all his house's wealth for her clothes. . . . It is easiest for the man who has a nonentity, but a woman sitting at home in silliness is harmful. I hate clever women. There will never be a woman in my house who is cleverer than a woman should

be. For Aphrodite brings more evildoing to birth in the clever ones. But the helpless woman is deprived of folly by her small wits. A servant ought never to go near a woman, but mute beasts ought to live with her, so that she has no one to talk to or to take messages back from her. (Eur. *Hipp.* 617–48)

Greek misogyny in the passage recur[s] with impressive constancy: woman is more dangerous the further away she is from the rule that would keep her silent and ignorant. For Hippolytus the woman should be stupid too, since only stupidity can keep the damage she causes to a minimum. The very bitterness of the attack leads one to assume an identification of Euripides with his character.

A REBELLION AGAINST WOMEN'S SUFFERING

But how may one explain the rebellion of another Euripidean character—Medea—from the fate reserved for women?

> Of everything that breathes and has intelligence, we women are the most miserable creatures. For first of all we must by a vast expenditure of wealth buy a husband and take a master for our bodies. And this evil is more miserable than the other, and everything depends on whether we get a bad master or a good one. For it is not respectable for women to be divorced or possible to refuse one's husband. A woman must be a seer when she finds herself among new habits and customs, since she will not have learned at home how she can best deal with her husband. And if, after we complete our work well, our husbands live with us bearing the yoke of marriage without constraint, our lives are enviable. If they do not, death is imperative. For a man, when he is miserable living with those inside his home, goes outside and puts an end to his heart's longing. . . . But we must look to one soul alone. They say that we lead a life without danger at home, while the men go to war—but they are wrong: I would rather stand in the hoplite ranks three times than give birth once. (Eur. *Med.* 230–51)

Medea does not lament a personal unhappiness nor does she weep about her individual fate—speaking in the name of all women, for the first time in Greek literature, she rebels against the sufferings of the female condition.

THE FEMALE QUESTION

The opposing positions of Hippolytus and Medea are unreconcilable, but the presence in Euripides' plays of two characters so emblematic, each in his or her own way, of extreme positions perhaps has a reason. The Athens of Euripides was the city of [the philosopher] Socrates [who

sions were both reflected and engendered in the plays of the period. In particular, the questioning of notions about the 'naturalness' of sexual divisions found an outlet in drama. The probing nature of this process means that no one play can be expected to present a unified and static view of female/male interactions; and this is even less feasible in relation to the dramatic corpus as a whole, which contains plays written by different authors at different historical moments.

MALE AND FEMALE BOUNDARY-CROSSERS

Nevertheless, the plays which deal with gender conflict share certain broad narrative devices. Often a situation is envisaged in which actions performed by male characters provoke an intrusion by women into the public arena, a turn of events which involves the assumption by the women of masculine modes of behaviour. This transgression of normal sexual boundaries on the part of the females is sometimes seen to result in a partial feminisation of the males. Sexual role-reversals of this kind are represented most explicitly in comedy, where they are accompanied by cross-dressing. But they are also present in tragedy, although here the emphasis is usually on the female side of the process— on the women's usurpation of masculine roles.

In the first play of Aeschylus's *Oresteia* trilogy, for example, the queen Clytemnestra is repeatedly represented as having behaved in a masculine fashion during her husband Agamemnon's lengthy absence at the Trojan War. . . . In Sophocles' tragedy *Antigone*, the heroine rebels against the law of the state by attempting to perform funeral rites for her dead brother, who in a decree introduced by her uncle King Creon has been refused burial on the grounds that he was a traitor. Antigone's sister Ismene pleads with her not to overstep the normal bounds of female behaviour: 'Remember we are women,/ we're not born to contend with men' (61–2); and Creon, justifying his refusal to pardon Antigone, urges that 'we must defend the men who live by law,'/ never let some woman triumph over us' (677–8). . . .

Euripides in his tragedy *Medea* envisages a conflict between female and male which is provoked by divergent attitudes to the marital bond. When her husband Jason abandons her so that he may make an advantageous marriage to a princess, Medea takes control of her own affairs with ruthless efficiency, and in plotting her revenge adopts a behavioural ethos conventionally associated with the archetypal male hero: 'Let no-one think of me/ as humble or weak or passive; let them understand/ I am of a different kind: dangerous to my enemies,/ Loyal to my friends. To such a life glory belongs' (807–10). If Medea had been a warrior going off to war, these words would have seemed admirable to most Athenians. The terrible irony of her declaration is that she is not about to fight a battle but to murder the princess, the princess's father and her own dearly loved children, because this is the most effective way she knows of punishing Jason. Medea's transgression of the sexual boundary involves adherence to a code of public morality which has horrific results when transported into the private sphere of existence. Jason, on the other hand, who stars elsewhere in myth as the classic he-man, is represented here as insensitive, calculating and rather stupid; he, of course, has been far from 'loyal to his friends'. In abandoning Medea, he has broken his oath, an essential item in the traditional hero's moral equipment. Medea however has remained true to hers —she has fulfilled her vow to win revenge.

Women are particularly prominent in the plays of Euripides, and a number of them in addition to *Medea* contain allusions to sexual boundary crossing. In *Hippolytus* (see pp. 31, 38–9), Phaedra's dreadful passion for her young stepson reduces her to a fevered state in which she longs to escape to the masculine environments of the hunt or the racetrack (*Hippolytus* 215–31). In *Electra*, Orestes seems hesitant and cautious when he returns from exile to win vengeance for his father's death, and it is his sister Electra who displays the resolution and conviction which one would expect of a hero. The *Bacchae* offers the most explicit allusions to role reversal. When the ecstatic women worshippers of Dionysus take to the hills, they abandon the conventional role allotted to females within the ordered culture of the city. . . .

This recurrent theme of sexual boundary-crossing may well represent an element deriving from the traditional religious framework for the performance of Athenian drama. Rituals in which men and women imitated each other in their dress and behaviour are known to have been a feature of a number of religious festivals, and they were also present in some of the initiation rites associated either with the onset of puberty or with marriage. The explanation which is usually offered for these practices is that they represented a

temporary assumption of an 'otherness' which social convention required one to banish from one's ordinary life, and
that the ritualised putting aside of this inverse role helped to
reinforce the unambiguous nature of one's subsequent sexual identity. This function of reinforcement could also be at-
tributed to a number of Athenian tragedies. On a superficial
level plays such as *Medea* or the *Bacchae* might easily be
seen as cautionary tales, designed to bring home the message that women who invade masculine areas of activity
wreak terrible havoc in their families and communities.
Some members of an Athenian audience may well have been
satisfied with this simple reading of the tragedies. But the
complex handling of the theme of role reversal precludes
single, exclusive interpretations. The multiplicity of meanings which it creates takes the theme far beyond its original
purpose of ritual reinforcement. . . .

The most explicit statement of the social repression experi-
enced by women is put into the mouth of Medea, who is im-
pelled by her husband's desertion into an embittered out-
pouring on the wrongs suffered by members of her sex
(230–58). 'Surely, of all creatures that have life and will, we
women/ Are the most wretched.' Women, she says, are forced
to accept as masters of their bodies men whose characters are
totally unknown to them. If the man turns out to be bad, his
wife cannot reject him, and divorce only brings disgrace. A
husband who is tired of his home can find diversions elsewhere, but a wife is compelled to look to one man alone. Nor
is her life free from danger, for marriage brings with it all the
perils of childbirth. The sympathy which Medea's plight
evokes in the chorus and in many members of the audience
at this point in the play is not entirely dissipated even at the
moment when the heroine is on the verge of murdering her
children. The playwright graphically represents the agonising
mental processes which Medea must go through before she
can steel herself to perform the deed (*Medea* 1021–80). The
fact that Euripides has been judged by modern critics to be
both a misogynist and a feminist is indicative of his multi-lay-
ered approach to his female characters. Medea is not the only
Euripidean woman who, while conforming to the ideological
stereotype of the dangerous and excessive female, is capable
at the same time of appearing justified in her actions.

To modern spectators of Greek drama the framing of
ideas about women may well appear to be the most signifi-

cant issue raised by these plays. Some people will applaud their acknowledgement of women's power, others will be horrified by the violence with which this power is so often associated. It is unlikely, however, that the dramatists themselves were consciously addressing 'the problem of women'. Their treatment of female characters must be viewed within the broader context of their construction of gender relations. . . . The clash between the sexes in Greek drama can be equated with a wider conflict between the public and private

MEDEA'S AGONY

This is the speech to which Professor Blundell refers, in which Medea agonizes over the dire deed she is about to perform.

MEDEA: O children, children! You have a city, and a home;
And when we have parted, there you both will stay for ever,
You motherless, I miserable. And I must go
To exile in another land, before I have had
My joy of you, before I have seen you growing up,
Becoming prosperous. I shall never see your brides,
Adorn your bridal beds, and hold the torches high.
My misery is my own heart, which will not relent.
All was for nothing, then—these years of rearing you,
My care, my aching weariness, and the wild pains
When you were born. Oh, yes, I once built many hopes
On you; imagined, pitifully, that you would care
For my old age, and would yourselves wrap my dead body
For burial. How people would envy me my sons!
That sweet, sad thought has faded now. Parted from you,
My life will be all pain and anguish. You will not
Look at your mother any more with these dear eyes.
You will have moved into a different sphere of life.

Dear sons, why are you staring at me so? You smile
At me—your last smile: why?
[*She weeps. The* CHILDREN *go from her a little, and she turns to the Chorus.*]
                    Oh, what am I to do?
Women, my courage is all gone. Their young, bright faces
I can't do it. I'll think no more of it. I'll take them
Away from Corinth. Why should I hurt *them*, to make
Their father suffer, when I shall suffer twice as much
Myself? I won't do it. I won't think of it again.

What is the matter with me? Are my enemies
To laugh at me? Am I to let them off scot free?

spheres—in Greek terms, between *polis* [community] and *oikos* [family]. When women cross the boundary between the male and female realms, they are often doing so in defence of the interests of the household, which are being threatened by actions performed by men in the public arena. . . .

In Euripides' *Medea*, the heroine is incensed by her husband's lack of personal loyalty, while Jason maintains that he has ended their marriage in order to secure, through his new alliance with the royal family, prosperity and public es-

I must steel myself to it. What a coward I am,
Even tempting my own resolution with soft talk.
Boys, go indoors.
[*The* CHILDREN *go to the door, but stay there watching her.*]
                If there is any here who finds it
Not lawful to be present at my sacrifice,
Let him see to it. My hand shall not weaken.

Oh, my heart, don't, don't do it! Oh, miserable heart,
Let them be! Spare your children! We'll all live together
Safely in Athens; and they will make you happy. . . . No!
No! No! By all the fiends of hate in hell's depths, no!
I'll not leave sons of mine to be the victims of
My enemies' rage. In any case there is no escape,
The thing's done now. Yes, now—the golden coronet
Is on her head, the royal bride is in her dress,
Dying, I know it. So, since I have a sad road
To travel, and send these boys on a still sadder road,
I'll speak to them. Come, children; give me your hand, dear
    son;
Yours too. Now we must say goodbye. Oh, darling hand,
And darling mouth; your noble, childlike face and body!
Dear sons, my blessing on you both—but there, not here!
All blessing here your father has destroyed. How sweet
To hold you! And children's skin is soft, and their breath
    pure.
Go! Go away! I can't look at you any longer;
My pain is more than I can bear.
           [*The* CHILDREN *go indoors.*]
                  I understand
The horror of what I am going to do; but anger,
The spring of all life's horror, masters my resolve.

Euripides, *Medea*, in Philip Vellacott, trans., *Euripides: Medea and Other Plays.* New York: Penguin Books, 1963, pp. 48–50.

teem for his sons (551–68). In plays such as these the public and private spheres are shown to be bound together by relations which are both reciprocal and oppositional. In focusing on the point of interaction between them, Athenian tragedy explores a set of contradictions for which Athenian law, by establishing public masculine control over private female behaviour, had attempted to find a simple solution. . . .

MEN'S AND WOMEN'S ROLES RE-ASSESSED

[Scholar of ancient women F.I.] Zeitlin has argued that Athenian drama was an institution designed primarily for the education of male citizens in a democratic state, and that the prominence of the feminine principle in the theatre has to be analysed in this context. Women, she believes, are being represented not for their own sake, but because of what they reveal about the male identity. Zeitlin rightly points out that women characters regularly serve as the catalysts through which the consequences of male actions are made to rebound on to their original perpetrators: women's sufferings generally lead to disasters which occur before those of the males and help to precipitate them. It is because 'the woman is assigned the role of the radical other' that she can be used in this way to examine and reconstruct male behaviour and values. This function is underlined by the ritual aspects of Greek theatre. Women literally did not represent themselves in Greek drama, but were impersonated by male actors; and theatrical space was dominated by the public arena of the orchestra and the stage, while the house, the feminine sphere, remained hidden and mysterious.

As Zeitlin suggests, the otherness of women is a prominent aspect of tragic drama, one that complicates the challenge to public values which females represent. When women break out of the domestic interior, they tend to pass not merely into the public arena but also beyond it, entering the realms which exist beyond the civilisation and order of the *polis*. . . . Medea's otherness is also demonstrated by her foreignness, which she herself stresses at the end of her 'wrongs of women' speech (252–8), and by her skills as a sorceress. In addition, many of these women have strong links with the divine realm of being. Clytemnestra can be seen on one level as an instrument of divine retribution . . . Antigone believes herself to be acting in defence of unwritten laws ordained by the gods . . . and the actions of the Bacchae

are the medium through which the power of the god Dionysus is demonstrated. Medea, as so often, provides the most
striking example: at the conclusion of the play she is swept
away to safety in the chariot of her grandfather, the Sun-god.

The relationships which all these women bear to spheres —
natural, foreign or divine—which exist beyond the boundaries
of male political order provide another reason why gender conflict cannot be reduced to a simple clash between private and
public. Private experience is only one of the hidden dimensions
which men are forced to confront when they are opposed by
women. This analysis tends to confirm Zeitlin's notion of
drama as an essentially male project. The focus is on the masculine sense of identity and the crises which it undergoes when
the boundaries it has created are undermined. The masculine
polis invents itself by establishing what it is not—by construct-
ing areas of difference and separating them off from itself. The
women who represent these differences erupt into the *polis*
from the inside—from the domestic interior—but also from the
realms which exist on the outside. When boundaries are
crossed in this way they may be re-established or they may be
moved. In either case they are re-assessed.

A Dramatization of the Problems of Domestic Life

Werner Jaeger

Scholars often point out Euripides' tendency to create less formal and more realistic characters and situations in his works. In this excerpt from his famous
book, *Paideia: The Ideals of Greek Culture,* the
renowned German classicist Werner Jaeger argues
that Euripides' realism was, at least for his place and
time, often bourgeois in character, that is, involved
with middle-class ideas and problems of everyday
people. Thus, though Medea and Jason are decidedly
upper-class by birth, a good many of the problems
they encounter and endure—infidelity, marital discord, spouse abuse, child custody, and so on—are like
those of ordinary people. And in this way the play dra-
matizes some of the realities of domestic life, then and
now, albeit through the use of formal, stylized language and staging.

When Euripides came forward to compete for the tragedian's prize, and presented mythical dramas in what appeared to be severely conservative form, he was unable to
convince his audience that his own innovations were only a
further step in the current tendency to humanize and mod-
ernize the myths.

EXPANDING THE LIMITS OF ORDINARY REALITY

He must have known that he was a true revolutionary; his
contemporaries were profoundly disturbed or violently dis-
gusted by his work. Clearly Greek sentiment was more prepared to see the myths converted into a set of . . . conventional ideals, as they had almost become in . . . much of the
elaborate choric poetry of the sixth century, than expanded

Excerpted from Werner Jaeger, *Paideia: The Ideals of Greek Culture,* translated by
Gilbert Highet. Reprinted with permission from Blackwell Publishers.

and transformed to fit the categories of ordinary reality, which bore the same relation to mythology as the profane [everyday, non-spiritual] world to the world of religion and the spirit nowadays. Nothing is so characteristic of the naturalistic trend of that age as the effort made by its artists to keep mythology from becoming empty and remote, by revising its standards to suit the facts of real life viewed without illusion. Euripides attacked this strange new task, not in cold blood, but with the passionate energy of a strong artistic personality, and with unshaken perseverance in the face of many years of defeat and discouragement. It was long before the Athenian people gave him any considerable support; yet he won in the end, and dominated not only the Athenian stage but the whole Hellenic world. . . .

In him, as in every other truly living Greek poet, literary form grows organically out of one definite material: it is inseparable from it, and is often conditioned by it even in such minor details as the formation of words and the pattern of sentences. His new material transformed not only the myths but even the poetic language he inherited and the traditional form of tragedy—for Euripides did not break up that form out of mere caprice [sudden impulse], but rather tended to fix it in a rigid schematism [pattern or system]. The new elements which formed his style, then, were *bourgeois realism, rhetoric* [the art of persuasive speech] and *philosophy*. The stylistic revolution which they brought about marked a great epoch in the history of the human mind, for it prefigured the future dominance of the three great cultural forces of later Hellenism [Greek culture]. In every scene of his plays it is evident that his work presupposed a particular cultural level and addressed a special type of society; and, on the other hand, that it was the true guide which helped the new type of human character to find itself, by showing it the ideal which it hoped to approach, and which it needed, perhaps more than in any previous era, for its own self-justification.

A COMPLETELY UP-TO-DATE PLAY

The encroachment of *bourgeois ideals* upon life meant to Euripides' contemporaries something the same as the encroachment of proletarian ideals [those of the workers of the poorer classes] to us: in fact, it often verged on proletarianization, as when Euripides brought miserable ragged beggars on the stage to represent the tragic heroes of antiquity. That was just the type of debasement which his opponents most violently attacked. Even in *Medea*, which is nearest in tone and spirit to the work of his predecessors, it can be traced throughout. As the individual citizen gained more and more political and intellectual freedom, the problems of human society and of the constraints on which it depends grew more obvious; men began to claim the right to live their own lives, wherever they felt themselves held down by artificial restraints; they attempted to find mitigation [relief] or escape by the use of reason. Marriage was hotly discussed. The relation of the sexes, which had for centuries been guarded by the tabu of convention, was now dragged into the light of day, and scrutinized, and found to be a conflict like every other relation in nature. Was it not governed by the right of the stronger, like them all? So the poet found the passions of his own day in the age of Jason's desertion of Medea, and infused into it problems unknown to the original myth, embodying them in the mighty lineaments of true tragedy.

The Athenian women of Euripides' time were not Medeas: they were too cultivated to play her part or else too dull and repressed. But the poet deliberately chose to write of Medea, the wild-eyed savage who murdered her children to injure her treacherous husband: for she expressed the elemental nature of woman untrammelled by Greek conventions. He presented Jason, whom the Greeks generally felt to be a blameless hero though not perhaps an ideal husband, as a cowardly opportunist, acting not from passion but from cold calculation. But that transformation was necessary to make the mythical murderess into a truly tragic figure. Euripides gave her all his sympathy: partly because he felt that the fate of women was sad, and could not see it glorified by mythology with its splendid heroic atmosphere of masculine prowess and masculine glory; and chiefly because he wished to make her the heroine of a domestic tragedy of bourgeois life, such as must often have occurred, although not in such an extreme form, in the Athens of his own time. Euripides invented domestic drama. *Medea*, with its conflict between the boundless egoism of the husband and the boundless passion of the wife, was a completely up-to-date play. Accordingly, the disputes, the abuse, and the logic used by all its characters are essentially bourgeois. Jason is stiff

with cleverness and magnanimity; while Medea philoso-
phizes on the social position of women—the dishonourable
necessity which makes a woman surrender herself in marriage to a strange man and pay a rich dowry for the privilege—and declares that bearing children is far more brave
and dangerous than fighting in battle. It is impossible for us
to admire the play wholeheartedly; yet it was a revolution in
its time, and it shows the true fertility of the new art.

CHAPTER 3

Medea and Other Major Characters

READINGS ON
MEDEA

The Characters Are Brilliantly Drawn

Gilbert Norwood

One of Euripides' greatest skills was creating characters of depth and color who, though presented in a stylistic setting, closely resemble people from everyday life. Here from his widely read study of Greek tragedy, Gilbert Norwood, a noted authority on the subject, briefly analyzes the three major characters of *Medea*—Medea, Jason, and Creon. His description of Jason's "self-centered stupidity" and "shameless brutality" is particularly apt and well worded.

The dramatic structure of the *Medea* calls for the closest attention. In Sophocles we have observed how that collision of wills and emotions, which is always the soul of drama, arises from the confrontation of two persons. In the present drama that collision takes place in the bosom of a single person. Sophocles would probably have given us a Jason whose claim upon our sympathy was hardly less than that of Medea. Complication, with him, is to be found in his plots, not in his characters. But here we have a subject which has since proved so rich a mine of tragic and romantic interest— the study of a soul divided against itself. Medea's wrongs, her passionate resentment, and her plans of revenge do not merely dominate the play, they *are* the play from the first line to the close. . . .

A STUDY IN FEMALE HUMAN NATURE

The characterization shows Euripides at his best. In the heroine he gives us the first and possibly the finest of his marvellous studies in feminine human nature. . . . Medea he has imagined from within. Her passionate love, which is so easily perverted by brutality into murderous hate, her pride, will-power, ferocity, and daemonic energy, are all depicted

Excerpted from Gilbert Norwood, *Greek Tragedy* (London, Methuen, 1920).

with flawless mastery and sympathy. Desperate and cruel as this woman shows herself, she is no cold-blooded plotter. Creon has heard of her unguarded threats, and his knowledge wellnigh ruins her project. Her first words to Jason, "thou utter villain," followed by a complete and appalling indictment of his cynicism and ingratitude, are not calculated to lull suspicion. But however passionate, she owns a splendid intellect. She faces facts and understands her weaknesses. When seeking an advantage, she can hold herself magnificently in hand. The pretended reconciliation with Jason is a scene of weird thrill for the spectators. Her archness in discussing his influence over the young princess is almost hideous, and while she weeps in his arms we remember with sick horror her scornful words after practising successfully the same arts on the king. Above all, there is here no petulant railing at "unjust gods," or "blind fate". Her

JASON'S SHAMELESSNESS

This early exchange between Jason and Medea immediately reveals what Professor Norwood calls Jason's "shameless brutality" in first abandoning his wife and children and then, in this scene, telling her to her face that he means her no harm and still cares about her. Medea minces no words in calling him a coward and reminding him of how he has stabbed her in the back.

JASON: I have often noticed—this is not the first occasion—
  What fatal results follow from ungoverned rage.
  You could have stayed in Corinth, still lived in this house,
  If you had quietly accepted the decisions
  Of those in power. Instead, you talked like a fool; and now
  You are banished. Well, your angry words don't upset *me;*
  Go on as long as you like reciting Jason's crimes.
  But after your abuse of the King and the princess
  Think yourself lucky to be let off with banishement.
  I have tried all the time to calm them down; but you
  Would not give up your ridiculous tirades against
  The royal family. So, you're banished. However, I
  Will not desert a friend. I have carefully considered
  Your problem, and come now, in spite of everything,
  To see that you and the children are not sent away
  With an empty purse, or unprovided. Exile brings
  With it a train of difficulties. You no doubt
  Hate me: but I could never bear ill-will to you.

undoing in the past has come from trust in the words of a man that is a Greek"; her present murderous rage springs from . . . her own passion. The dramatist has set himself to express human life in terms of humanity.

Jason is a superb study—a compound of brilliant manner, stupidity, and cynicism. If only his own desires, interests, are safe, he is prepared to confer all kinds of benefits. The kindly, breezy words which he addresses to his little sons must have made hundreds of excellent fathers in the audience feel for a moment a touch of personal baseness—"am I not something like this?" That is the moral of Jason and countless personages of Euripides: they are so detestable and yet so like ourselves. Jason indeed dupes himself as well as others. He really thinks he is kind and gentle, when he is only surrendering to an emotional atmosphere. His great weakness is the mere perfection of his own egotism; he has

---

MEDEA: You filthy coward!—if I knew any worse name
For such unmanliness I'd use it—so, you've come!
You, my worst enemy, come to me! Oh, it's not courage,
This looking friends in the face after betraying them.
It is not even audacity; it's a disease,
The worst a man can have, pure shamelessness. However,
It is as well you came; to say what I have to say
Will ease my heart; to hear it said will make you wince.

I will begin at the beginning. When you were sent
To master the fire-breathing bulls, yoke them, and sow
The deadly furrow, then I saved your life; and that
Every Greek who sailed with you in the Argo knows.
The serpent that kept watch over the Golden Fleece,
Coiled round it fold on fold, unsleeping—it was I
Who killed it, and so lit the torch of your success.
I willing deceived my father; left my home;
With you I came to Iolcus by Mount Pelion,
Showing much love and little wisdom. There I put
King Pelias to the most horrible of deaths
By his own daughters' hands, and ruined his whole house.
And in return for this you have the wickedness
To turn me out, to get yourself another wife,
Even after I had borne you sons!

Euripides, *Medea,* in Philip Vellacott, trans., *Euripides: Medea and Other Plays.*
New York: Penguin Books, 1963, pp. 30–31.

no power at all to realize another's point of view. Throughout the play he simply refuses to believe that Medea feels his
desertion as she asserts. For him her complaints are "empty
words". To the very end his self-centered stupidity is almost
pathetic: "didst thou *in truth* determine on their death for the
sake of wifely honour?" One of the most deadly things in the
play hangs on this blindness. Medea has just asked him,
with whatever smile she can summon up, to induce "your
wife" to procure pardon for the children. Jason, instead of
destroying himself on the spot in self-contempt, replies
courteously: "By all means; and I imagine that I shall persuade her, *if she is like the rest of women*". Considering all
circumstances, this is perhaps unsurpassed for shameless
brutality. Medea, however, with a gleam in her eye which
one may imagine, answers with equal urbanity, even with
quiet raillery. She has perhaps no reason to complain; it is
precisely this portentous insensibility which will secure her
success.

The minor characters are, in their degree, excellently
drawn—Creon above all. His short scene is unforgettable; it
is that familiar sight—a weak man encouraging himself to
firmness by exaggerating his own severity. His delicious little grumble, "my chivalrous instincts have got me into trouble more often than I like to think of," stamps him as the
peer of Dogberry and Justice Shallow [noted Shakespearean
characters who are both pompous and weak minded].

Medea the Master Manipulator

Eleanor Wilner

One of the most striking aspects of Medea's character is her ability to manipulate others, something she
does in scene after scene. Eleanor Wilner, who has
taught at the Universities of Hawaii and Chicago and
who recently translated *Medea* for the Penn Greek
Drama Series, here examines Medea's two-faced-
ness. Wilner calls her a Machiavel, that is, a person
in the same mold as the manipulative, amoral ruler
depicted in fifteenth-century Italian writer Niccolo
Machiavelli's famous book, *The Prince*. She also
makes the point that this sort of self-absorbed, arro-
gant, and morally neutral character bears some
striking and disturbing resemblances to many
people in the modern world.

The Chorus, Jason, Creon, and Medea all mouth pieties their
actions or their next speech belie. The difference between
Medea and the other characters in this regard is that she is
aware of her (and their) duplicity, and uses that awareness
to manipulate the others. She knows well the weaknesses
their vaunted or pious words conceal—and plays on the particular vanities of each character. She is a Machiavel without
a country to rule—her cause is her own injured pride and
power, and the tragedy of Medea, if tragedy is indeed the
right word for this brand of truth, is not only that her scale is
outsize for the scope of her role in life, but that the logic of the
perfect revenge of the cornered person has a Samson-like
side—her revenge is surgically exquisite, her enemies are destroyed, and, in a manner of speaking, she has pulled down
the house on her own head [a reference to the biblical character Samson, the strong-man who toppled the temple of his
enemies, the Philistines, destroying himself in the process].

Excerpted from Eleanor Wilner, "Translator's Preface: *Medea*" in *Euripides, 1,* edited
by David R. Slavitt and Palmer Bovie. Copyright © 1998 University of Pennsylvania
Press. Reprinted with permission from the publisher. All rights reserved.

Her house had, of course, been her cage, even as her sense of humiliation was sharpened by her circumstantial dependence on a hollow man into whom her passionate nature and thwarted power once poured full force, a husband for whom she has obvious and, we can surmise, longstanding contempt. From such a power imbalance—she having the innate, he the institutionalized power—comes the time-honored saying "Hell hath no fury like a woman scorned." To understand that, it is necessary to hear simultaneously under that last phrase another—"like a woman's scorn." It surfaces in Medea's clear statement of the purpose of all this blood: "But what is grief compared to the ridicule of fools?"

The . . . chill of those words reaches the bone when we recall the spilled blood from which that grief arises. The dead children are both fact and metaphor, for on what future, what innocence or principle or hero can the audience now rely? At the end of the *Medea* the future seems empty, almost unimaginable—and it is perhaps that, as much as its psychological acuity, which makes the play seem so unfortunately appropriate to our own moment. There is, as well, the equally appropriate fact that her connections with the past have twice been savagely cut by Medea's own hand, and this for the sake of her passion. In this she may be the Western original for that person who has become all too familiar to us today—the radically disconnected self pursuing personal desires in an egocentric universe.

The servants in the play—nurse, tutor, messenger—are the reliable characters, which only sharpens the bitter ironies, for they function in the play as the predictors and reliable narrators of events to which they are powerless witnesses, crimes at which they express horror but are entirely helpless to prevent. The Chorus? To the traditional caution of Greek citizen Choruses, they add a mean-spirited self-interest and barely hidden animus which are, in their way, almost as repellent as the opportunistic cowardice of Jason or the calculated crimes of the outraged and raging Medea. The very first words from the Chorus warn us of the way people take pleasure in the pain of others, and may alert us to one of the assumptions on which Euripides rests his dramaturgy, and which may be one explanation for the play's enduring popularity. Hearing the wailing cries emerge from Medea's house, they allow as how they can't take pleasure in the fall of this house, as they "have shared the cup of friendship there." There is loyalty there, yes, but also this first, and seemingly unwitting revelation of sadistic excitement as a commonplace.

The Chorus reveal themselves more fully as the play goes on, slowly sacrificing an unvexed sympathy we might feel for them as women making common cause with a wounded, betrayed sister. Consider, for instance, when Medea, ignoring their pleas, goes into her house, resolved to murder her children. What do the Chorus say in response to this impending crime? They talk about the luck of those who never had children, how much trouble child-rearing is, how uncertain its outcome, and so on and so forth. Here I am, their translator, more than a little aghast, expecting floods of outrage and sorrow at the deed Medea is about to do. And what I find instead is a weird paean to the blessings of the barren, who will never know the burdens of raising ungrateful, unemployable, or, should they turn out well, mortal children.

What kind of poorly disguised identification is going on between these women and the one about to butcher her young? Even to us post-moderns schooled in the acceptance of ambivalence [uncertainty about which course to follow], this response is wrenching in its inappropriateness to the extremity of the situation, making the Chorus callous and obliquely complicit. And when the messenger recounts in graphic, sickening detail the atrocious death of the young princess and the old king, "a sight," he says, "to wring tears from a stone," the only response of the dry-eyed Chorus is to ignore the victims and say, self-righteously, that Jason has deserved these disasters.

The uneasiness about their stance is brought by Euripides to an acute edge when, during those terrible moments when the children are actually being killed and cry out for help, he has the Chorus protest that they should not allow this to continue; they seem about to intervene—and then . . . they do absolutely nothing. They are paralyzed all but linguistically—as if the rift between word and deed has become an acknowledged and visible chasm, and shame has fled the earth, as the Chorus had said of Jason's perfidy in an earlier ode when their pious eloquence was still convincing:

The sacred oath, its power,
is overthrown,
and shame from Hellas flown—
she has taken wing for high Olympus,
where she hides her face in cloud.

A REVERSAL OF CHARACTER TYPES

Many of Medea's speeches are righteous, too, often genuinely so, as if constantly to remind us that the best causes
can have the worst representatives or succumb to vile actions, and that to wound people is not to make them the
great human beings our sympathies for the injustices done
to them would have them be, but rather to damage them and
make them vengeful. That the most ardent and articulate
statement in the Classical tradition of the evils to which a
woman's lot subjects her comes from the mouth of a figure
who has already committed abhorrent acts (including the
murder of her own brother to forward her lover's ambitions)
and will soon commit worse ones, is to undermine any
moral clarity that could be put to political uses. By making
Medea the murderer of her own children, which scholarly
consensus now considers Euripides' original alteration of
the accepted version (in which the Corinthians killed the
children to avenge the murder of their ruling family), he not
only turns tragic action to horror show but makes finally
impossible any sense of Medea's moral agency.

Equally in her passion, her intelligence, her pride, her
powers, her ability to bend others to her will, her blood relationship to a god, her ruthless determination to destroy her
enemies, her refusal ever to play the victim, Medea embod-
ies qualities admired in the male ruler or hero, and her ap-
propriation of those qualities in the play ironically shows
them for what they most brutally are. . . .

Medea makes this double standard explicit in a soliloquy
which she ends with these words:

> . . . Take heart, Medea,
> use all your arts, inquire of all you know, and all you are—
> spare nothing. For what they did to you—those sons of double-
> dealing, false-speaking Sisyphus—foul murder is a fair re-
> turn. Have the courage of your kind: the seed of gods
> spawned you—the offspring of a noble father, and Helios, the
> sun himself, your grandsire. Fire is your element; you know
> what you must do. Well, we are women, aren't we, our best
> designs have made us architects of harm, for deeds of glory
> are denied to us—so we must do our worst.

That her worst, when mounted and armored and *his*, is traditionally called glorious is one of the great unmasking
truths of this play. The anger of Achilles has a different playing field from the anger of Medea, and Euripides seems
guided here by a gaunter muse than Homer or his descen-

dants, producing an art in which truth is far from coincident with beauty, and the Grecian urn is filled with ashes. To complete the inversion [reversal] of types, Euripides portrays the Ur-Greek hero Jason as a shallow, opportunistic, and self-deluded cad, who owes his hero's reputation—as Medea rightfully reminds him—to her wiles and powers, rather than to his own strength.

Both the one large and the many small figures seem designed to unmask the heroic, and to confront the audience with the pettiness, vanity, hypocrisy, selfishness, violence and impotent rationality of humankind, a smallness magnified by high position. The one large and towering figure whose perverse use of her own powers and her ability to strip the self-glorifying masks from others (which becomes most horrifyingly literal in the burning off of the beauty of Jason's princess-bride by playing on her vanity) makes Medea's very magnificence, its heroism if you will, a mockery of the vileness of her means to assert her superior power, and the littleness to which such towering passion and pride will stoop. As if to measure the loss of Greek balance, disproportion is everywhere.

THE WORST SOMETIMES OVERTAKES THE BEST

I was struck, as I translated, by the petty domestic squabbling of Jason and Medea, a point-scoring contest that is resumed even in the final scene over the bodies of their children. Here Euripides seemed intent on showing the dialogue form reduced to mere bickering, degrading the form which Greek philosophy and political debate brought to a high pitch. Equally striking are the relentless egoism and manipulative intent of Medea's arguments, so that her justly famous speech about women's lot is spoken to win the Corinthian women to her side and to bind them to secrecy, even as her brilliant unmasking of the rhetorical sophistries of rationalizing, specious [hollow] argument in relation to Jason seems equally to be a smokescreen for her own more adroit [skillful] use of such logical tricks.

Both Creon and especially Jason she manipulates with wheedling and flattery that are so uncharacteristic as to send off warnings to all but the most self-deluded; Aegeus of Athens, too, she plays like a lyre to her own desire's tune. And the speech in which she hesitates at the brink of child-murder and supposedly bares a mother's tender heart is itself almost completely self-absorbed. She thinks not of what she is taking from her children but of what she will lose, all the mother's prerogatives she will be abdicating, and, in a stunning flight of self-pity, she imagines herself in old age, newly dead, her children lovingly washing her body in a tender finale which she will be denying herself by killing them.

This nihilistic play [i.e., one lacking any traditional moral compass]—its glories of eloquence and insight calculated, like the speeches of Medea that twist her listeners to her purposes, to set us up for the cruelty of disillusion, moral disproportion, and disappointed expectation of order—is the one which the times and the task of translation revealed to me. The Chorus' epilogue itself reinforces this reading, and, with a final ironic reversion to piety, attributes the outcome to Zeus. Indeed, it is the dragon chariot of her grandfather Helios, the Sun, that carries Medea triumphantly off over the heads of the Corinthians—another slaughter of the innocents underwritten by the gods, a divine sanction unacceptable to the reverent critics. What could Euripides have meant? they have asked repeatedly. Surely this must be regarded as a failure of dramatic art, this *deus ex machina* a clumsy device. But what if the ending is entirely consistent with the play's central intentions? In the process of translation, watching the play's cruel actions erase their own extenuation, the question again arose—if the pieties of the critics but drape this anatomizing of cold rage in the face of pettiness and betrayal, to what does this play owe its longevity, and even, in relation to the other Classical Greek tragedies, its exceptional and enduring popularity?

The answer to that, though it can be neither single nor simple, attests perhaps to certain unpalatable truths about ourselves (more overt and inescapable at certain places and times than others), truths which Euripides both appeals to and enacts in *Medea.* In this, our century of atrocities—of mass murder on an unprecedented and emotionally numbing scale—one truth is undeniable: that the worst sometimes overtakes the best in people, and that insanely murderous and ultimately self-ruinous "solutions" may be chosen over saner ones, even when we know better. Medea articulates this in these despairing lines: "rage will bite through reason's curb—how useless to know / that the worst harm comes to us from heedless wrath."

Medea as a Classic Tragic Hero

Bernard Knox

At first glance, most people today would likely be perplexed and disturbed at calling a mother who kills her children a hero. But this stems from the common modern vision of a hero as the embodiment of "good" (and, by natural contrast, the villain as the embodiment of "evil"). In ancient Greek mythology and literature, especially as delineated by Euripides' senior colleague, Sophocles in his *Oedipus Tyrannos* (*Oedipus the King*), a hero was an individual who possessed a firmness of purpose more intense and steadfast than that of ordinary people. The hero had his own ideal vision of what was right and never swerved from that vision. And in making that vision a reality, he routinely aided his friends and destroyed his enemies, in the process committing some acts that, in and of themselves, modern spectators might find brutal, pitiless, and/or mean-spirited. Thus, a hero was not necessarily always "good" in the modern sense of the word. In this well-informed, thoughtful essay, the renowned classical scholar Bernard Knox makes the case that, despite the despicable act of killing her own children, Medea fulfills the definition of a tragic hero in the Sophoclean sense. And this, he says, shows Euripides' brilliance as a dramatic innovator—that in making a woman, and worse, a murderess, a hero, he broke the mold and expanded the scope of the dramatic art.

Medea . . . is presented to us, from the start, in heroic terms. Her language and action, as well as the familiar frame in which they operate, mark her as a heroic character, one of those great individuals whose intractable firmness of pur-

Excerpted from Bernard Knox, *Work and Action: Essays on the Ancient Theater*, pp. 297–303. Copyright © 1979. Reprinted with permission from The Johns Hopkins University Press.

pose, whose defiance of threats and advice, whose refusal to betray their ideal vision of their own nature, were the central preoccupation of Sophoclean tragedy. The structure and language of the *Medea* is that of the Sophoclean heroic play. This is the only extant Euripidean tragedy constructed according to the model which Sophocles was to perfect in the *Oedipus Tyrannos* and which, through the influence of that supreme dramatic achievement . . . became the model for Renaissance and modern classical tragedy: the play dominated by a central figure who holds the stage throughout, who initiates and completes—against obstacles, advice and threats—the action, whether it be discovery or revenge. Other Euripidean tragedies are different. *Hippolytus* is a drama with four principal characters. Hecuba, who is on stage throughout *The Trojan Women*, is no dominating figure but a passive victim, as she is also in the play named after her, until she turns into a revengeful Medea figure at the end. Pentheus, Heracles, and Andromache are victims rather than actors. Electra in her own play comes nearest to Medea in stage importance, but she cannot act without Orestes, and in the *Orestes* he shares the stage with her. . . . The *Medea* is the only Euripidean tragedy (in the modern sense of that word) which is tightly constructed around a "hero": a central figure whose inflexible purpose, once formed, nothing can shake—a purpose which is the mainspring of the action.

A Hero's Language and Style

Medea is presented to the audience in the unmistakable style and language of the Sophoclean hero. . . . She has the main characteristic of the hero, the determined resolve, expressed in uncompromising terms: the verbal adjectives *ergasteon* (791), "the deed must be done," and *tolmeteon* (1051) "I must dare"; the decisive futures—especially *kteno*, "I shall kill"—this word again and again. The firmness of her resolve is phrased in the customary Sophoclean terms *dedoktai* (1236), *dedogmenon* (822)—"my mind is made up." She is deaf to persuasion; she will not hear, *akouei* (29). She is moved by the typical heroic passions, anger, *orge* (176 etc.), wrath, *cholos* (94 etc.). She exhibits the characteristic heroic temper daring, *tolma* (394 etc.), and rashness, *thrasos* (856 etc.). She is fearful, terrible, *deine* (44 etc.) and wild, like a beast, *agrios* (193 etc.). She is much concerned, like the heroes, for her glory . . . she will not put up with injustice . . . and with what she regards as intolerable. . . . Above all, she is full of passionate intensity, that *thumos* which in her case is so marked a feature of her make-up that in her famous monologue she argues with it, pleads with it for mercy, as if it were something outside herself. Like the heroes, she feels that she has been treated with disrespect, *etimasmene* (20), *atimasas* (1354 etc.); wronged, *edikemene* (26 etc.); and insulted, *hubriz'* (603 etc.). Her greatest torment is the thought that her enemies will laugh at her, *gelos* (383 etc.). Like the Sophoclean heroes, she curses her enemies (607 etc.) while she plans her revenge. She is alone, *mone* (513) and abandoned, *eremos* (255 etc.), and in her isolation and despair she wishes for death.

Like the Sophoclean tragic hero, she resists alike appeals for moderation and harsh summonses to reason. She is admonished, *nouthetoumene* (29) by her friends but pays no more attention than a rock or the sea waves. She is begged to "consider," *skepsai* (851), but to no avail: she cannot be persuaded, *peithesthai* (184) or ruled, *archesthai* (120). The chorus beg her as suppliants, *hiketeuomen* (854) to change her mind, but to no effect. To others her resolution seems to be stupidity, folly, *moria* (457 etc.), and self-willed stubbornness, *authadia* (621); she is like a wild animal, a bull (92 etc.), a lioness (187 etc.).

As in Sophoclean heroic tragedy, there is also a secondary figure whose pliability under pressure throws the hero's unbending will into high relief. It is not, in this play, a weak sister . . . but a man . . . Creon; he is king of Corinth. He comes on stage, his mind made up: he has proclaimed sentence of immediate exile for Medea. She must leave at once: he is afraid of her. Her eloquent appeal falls on deaf ears: his resolve, he says, is fixed, *arare* (322). She will never persuade him. . . . But she does. He yields, though he knows that he is making a mistake, and gives her one more day.

MEDEA'S GRAND DESIGN

However, the structure of the *Medea* does differ from that of the Sophoclean hero play in one important respect: the hero . . . must conceal her purpose from everyone else in the play, except, of course, the chorus, whom . . . she must win over to her side. Consequently, a characteristically Sophoclean scene is missing: the two-actor dialogue in which the heroic resolve is assailed by persuasion, threat, or both. . . . But there *is* a speech in the *Medea* which rolls out all the clichés of the appeal to reason, the summons to surrender which, in Sophocles, all the heroes have to face. It is typical of Euripides' originality, of the way he makes things new, that this speech is delivered by Medea herself.

It is her false declaration of submission to Jason, her fulsome confession that she was only a foolish emotional woman, the speech that lures him to his doom. "I talked things over with myself," she tells him, "and reproached myself bitterly." As she reports her self-rebuke, she pulls out all the stops of the Sophoclean summons to reason. "Why do I act like a mad woman and show hostility to good advice? Shall I not rid myself of passion? I realize that my judgment was bad. . . . I raged in pointless anger . . . I was mindless. . . . I confess I was full of bad thoughts then . . . but have come to better counsel now. My anger has subsided." And later, when Jason accepts her apologies, she says, "I shall not disobey you. What you did was best for me."

Jason is understanding and sympathetic. "I congratulate you on your present frame of mind—and I don't blame you for things past. Anger is something you have to expect from a woman. . . . But your mind has changed for the better." As he turns from Medea to his sons, Euripides puts in his mouth a subtle variation on a Sophoclean theme: the threat to the hero that he or she will realize the need for surrender in time. . . . "You have realized what the best decision is," he says to her, "though it took time." He has swallowed the bait—hook, line, and sinker: the way is now prepared for the murders that will wreck his life.

This speech is part of Medea's grand design; these formulas of dissuasion masquerading as terms of submission are the instruments of her revenge. As if this were not a sufficiently daring adaptation of the patterns of the heroic play, Euripides presents us with another. There *is* one person who can and does pose a real obstacle to Medea's plans, who can effectively confront her with argument—Medea herself. In the monologue she delivers after she hears that her fatal gifts have been delivered into the princess's hands by her children, she pleads with herself, changes her mind, and changes again and then again to return finally and firmly to her intention to kill them. When the children look at her and smile, she loses her courage. "Farewell, my plans!" (1048).

But then she recovers. "Shall I earn the world's laughter by leaving my enemies unpunished? No, I must dare to do this!" (1049–51). Then a sudden surge of love and pity overcomes her again and she addresses herself to her own *thumos*, her passionate heroic anger, as if it were something outside herself. "Do not do it. Let them go, hard-hearted—spare the children!" (1056–57). But her *thumos* will not relent: the children must die. In this great scene the grim heroic resolve triumphs not over an outside adversary or adviser but over the deepest maternal feelings of the hero herself.

THE SIMPLE HEROIC CODE

This presentation in heroic terms of a rejected foreign wife, who was to kill her husband's new wife, the bride's father, and finally her own children, must have made the audience which saw it for the first time in 431 B.C. a trifle uneasy. Heroes, it was well known, were violent beings and since they lived and died by the simple code "help your friends and hurt your enemies" it was only to be expected that their revenges, when they felt themselves unjustly treated, dishonored, scorned, would be huge and deadly. The epic poems [i.e., Homer's *Iliad* and *Odyssey*] do not really question Achilles' right to bring destruction on the Greek army to avenge Agamemnon's insults, nor Odysseus' slaughter of the entire younger generation of the Ithacan aristocracy. Sophocles' Ajax sees nothing wrong in his attempt to kill the commanders of the army for denying him the armor of Achilles; his shame springs simply from his failure to achieve his bloody objective. But Medea is a woman, a wife and mother, and also a foreigner. Yet she acts as if she were a combination of the naked violence of Achilles and the cold craft of Odysseus, and, what is more, it is in these terms that the words of Euripides' play present her. "Let no one," she says, "think me contemptible and weak, nor inactive either, but quite the opposite—dangerous to my enemies, helpful to my friends. Such are the qualities that bring a life glory" (807ff.). It is the creed by which Homeric and Sophoclean heroes live—and die."

She is a hero, then, but since she is also a woman, she cannot prevail by brute strength; she must use deceit. She is, as she admits herself, a "clever woman," *sophe*, and this cleverness she uses to deceive everyone in the play, bending them to her frightful purpose. Creon is tricked into giving her one day's grace; she knows that his initial bluster hides a soft heart and fawns on him (her own term, *thopeusai* 368) to gain time. Aegeus is tricked into promising her asylum in Athens: tricked is the word, for if he had realized that she intended to destroy the royal house of Corinth and her own children, he would never have promised her protection. She knows this, and that is why she binds him by a solemn oath. And Jason she takes in completely by her assumption of the role of repentant wife: she showers him with such abject self-abasement, such fawning reiteration of all the male Greek clichés about women . . . that one wonders how Jason can believe it. But she knows her man. . . .

THE GODS ARE ON HER SIDE

And so the poisoned gifts are taken to the new bride; Medea, when she hears that they have been delivered and accepted, successfully resists the temptation to spare the children, and then, after savoring at length the messenger's frightful description of the poison's effects, she kills her sons. Her revenge is complete when Jason comes to save them; she holds their bodies in the chariot sent by her grandfather Helios, and, safe from Jason, taunts him with the wreck of all his hopes, his childlessness. The end of the play sees her leave to deposit the children's bodies in Hera's temple and then go off to Athens.

She triumphs. She will always suffer from the memory of what she did to the children, as she grudgingly admits to Jason (1361–62), but she has her full and exquisite revenge. "These children are dead," she says to him, "that is what will torment you" (1370). And she escapes the consequences of her action, and goes safely to Athens.

This is very unlike what happens to most Sophoclean heroes. Ajax triumphs in a way, but he is dead; Oedipus wins a kind of victory, but he is blind; Antigone's victory comes after she has hanged herself. This complete success of Medea is connected with another feature of the way she is presented which is also in sharp contrast with the Sophoclean hero. She is quite sure, from start to finish, that the gods are on her side.

All the Sophoclean heroes feel themselves, sooner or later, abandoned by gods as well as men: their loneliness is absolute, they can appeal only to the silent presence of mountains, sea, and air. But Medea from her first appearance has no doubts that the gods support her cause. She appeals to Themis (ancestral law) and Artemis (woman's help in childbirth!) to witness Jason's unjust action (160); she calls on Zeus, who, she says, knows who is responsible for her sorrows (332). . . . She asks Jason if he thinks the same gods by whom he swore fidelity no longer reign in power (493), appeals again to Zeus (516), and calls exultantly on "Zeus, the justice of Zeus and the light of the Sun" (764), as she sees her plans for revenge ensured by Aegeus' promise of shelter in Athens. After the murder of the children she is still confident, in her confrontation scene with Jason, that Zeus is on her side (1352), and she makes plans to deposit the bodies of her sons in the temple of Hera Akraia (1379). . . . She never wavers from her faith that what she does has divine approval. She can even say, to the messenger who brings the news from the palace which seals the fate of the children: "These things the gods and I, with my evil thoughts, have contrived.". . .

Euripides Defies Expectation

"The gods and I"—she sees herself as their instrument and associate. And the play gives us no reason to think that she is wrong. On the contrary, it confirms her claim in spectacular fashion. All through the play, appeals are made to two divine beings, Earth and Sun. It is by these divinities that Aegeus is made to swear the oath that he will protect Medea from her enemies once she reaches Athens; it is to Earth and Sun that the chorus appeals at the last moment, begging them to prevent the murder of the children, and Jason, in the last scene, asks Medea how, with her children's blood on her hands, she can look at Earth and Sun. "What Earth will do we shall not be told," but Helios, the Sun, is clearly on Medea's side. Not only are the poisoned gifts sent to the princess an inheritance from Helios (and the poison acts like a concentration of the sun's fire), but, more important, it is Helios who sends Medea the chariot on which she escapes to Athens. "In the gods' name," says Jason, "let me touch the soft skin of my sons" (1402–3). But *his* appeal to the gods has no effect; "Your words are wasted" (1404), Medea tells him, and draws away in her chariot as Jason appeals again to Zeus. The chorus ends the play with lines which appear in our manuscripts at the end of several other Euripidean plays; some critics have thought them inappropriate here, but they are obviously and squarely in their right place:

> Zeus on Olympus has many things in his store-room:
> the gods bring to pass many surprising things.
> What was expected is not fulfilled.
> For the unexpected the gods find a way.
> So this story turned out.

Medea's appearance as a heroic figure, as the murderer of her children who escapes the consequences of her actions, apparently with the blessing of the gods, must have seemed to the audience surprising beyond description. Euripides himself, like the gods, has many things in his store room; he has defied expectation and found a way for the unimagined.

CHAPTER 4

Later Adaptations and Productions of *Medea*

A Roman Version of *Medea* Sympathizes with Jason

Meyer Reinhold

Euripides' influence on later writers, especially play-wrights, was great. One of the first indications of this in antiquity was the fact that several Roman poets created their own versions of his plays, including *Medea*. The famous Roman poet Ovid (43 B.C. – ca. A.D. 17), for example, wrote a *Medea*, which unfortunately did not survive. One that did survive is the version by Lucius Annaeus Seneca (ca. 4 B.C. – A.D. 65), the brilliant philosopher and playwright who served for a while as an advisor to the notorious emperor Nero. (Seneca was so taken with Euripides that he wrote his own versions of five Euripidean plays.) In general, Seneca's version follows the original; however, in contrast to Euripides, who sympathizes (at least to some extent) with Medea and portrays Jason as an insincere weakling, Seneca clearly sympathizes with Jason, emphasizing that character's heroic image as it appears in the tale of the search for the Golden Fleece. Medea, in this version, is nothing more than a savage and dangerous barbarian who threatens the stability and harmony of civilized Greek life. Seneca also made some small but interesting changes in the play's ending, as seen in this synopsis of the play by Meyer Reinhold, a distinguished professor emeritus of Boston University.

This play is based on Euripides' *Medea*. But Seneca has introduced many innovations. The principal change is the shift of sympathy to Jason and the emphasis on the inhumanity of Medea. Seneca has transformed Euripides' play into a "blood and thunder" tragedy of revenge and a study in criminal psychology.

Excerpted from Meyer Reinhold, *Classical Drama, Greek and Roman.* Reprinted with permission from Barron's Educational Series, Inc.

ACT I

The scene is before the house of Medea in Corinth; nearby is the palace of King Creon. Medea, in a long monologue, shrieks for vengeance because Jason is deserting her to marry Creusa, the princess of Corinth. She prays to many gods and divine powers for death to the princess and Creon, and curses Jason, praying for a life of misery for him. She girds herself for horrible deeds of vengeance through her sorceress' skill.

The Chorus of Corinthian Men, sympathetic to Jason and hostile to Medea, sings a marriage song for Jason and Creusa. They pray for happiness for the bride and groom, and express their joy that Jason has been freed from wedlock with Medea.

ACT II

Medea is stirred to heights of fury by the marriage song. She elaborates on all she has done for Jason, including the crimes she committed for his sake—her betrayal of her father, the slaying of her brother, the destruction of Pelias. She loves Jason, and blames him for weakness in submitting to Creon's royal will. It is Creon she must punish. The Nurse seeks to calm her wrath, but Medea's fury mounts.

Creon enters. He would have Medea out of his realm at once, but has yielded to Jason's plea on her behalf. Creon fears her powers of witchcraft. She defends herself before Creon, reminding him of her royal descent, her help to the famous Greeks among the Argonauts, who came seeking the Golden Fleece in Colchis with Jason, her services to Jason. She begs him to return Jason to her, and asks for asylum in his kingdom. Creon defends Jason from complicity in her horrible crimes, and orders her out of his kingdom. All fear her, he declares, because she combines woman's deceit with the strength of a man. He will permit her children to remain, and will care for them. She begs for time to say farewell to her children. Creon grants her one day, and departs to attend the marriage.

The Chorus comments on the boldness of man in inventing ships, and his daring in sailing the seas. The first ship, the Argo, brought the Argonauts across the seas in their perilous voyage. The prizes they brought back were the Golden Fleece—and Medea. Seafaring has expanded the horizons of man to the East and West. In time there will be no more unknown lands.

ACT III

The Nurse tries to restrain Medea, who has been raging in mad fury. Medea wildly threatens terrible vengeance, and now begins to assail Jason.

Jason enters, declares his love for his children, and sincerely asserts they are his principal concern. Medea pours out her heart to Jason, pointing out the power and wealth she gave up to be with him, her difficult position as an exile,

---

JASON'S WEDDING SONG

This is part of the wedding song composed by Seneca for the end of Act I of his Medea *(as translated by Frank J. Miller), in which Jason marries Creon's daughter. A chorus of Corinthian men (in contrast with Euripides' chorus of Corinthian women) praises Jason, wishes him well, and expresses the hope that the "barbarous Colchian woman" named Medea will go away soon.*

Now on our royal nuptials graciously smiling,
Here may the lords of heaven and the deeps of the ocean
Come while the people feast in pious rejoicing!

First to the gods who sway the sceptre of heaven,
Pealing forth their will in the voice of thunder,
Let the white bull his proud head bow in tribute.

Then to the fair Lucina, her gift we offer,
White as the driven snow, this beautiful heifer,
Still with her neck untouched by the yoke of bondage. . . .

Thou who, on the marriage torches attending,
Night's dark gloom with favouring hand dispellest,
Hither come with languishing footstep drunken,
Binding thy temples fair with garlands of roses!

Star of the evening, thou who to twilight leadest
The day, and hailest again the dawn of the morning,
All too slowly thou com'st for lovers impatient,
Eager to see thy sign in the glow of the sunset. . . .

Now, O Jason, freed from the hateful wedlock
That held thee bound to the barbarous Colchian woman,
Joyfully wed the fair Corinthian maiden,
While at last her parents' blessings attend thee. . . .

Now let the bold and merry Fescennine laughter and jesting
Sound through our ranks. Let Medea fare in silence and darkness,
If perchance another lord she shall wed in her exile.

"Wedding Song for a Second Marriage," trans. Frank J. Miller, in Francis R.B. Godolphin, ed., *The Latin Poets.* New York: Random House, 1949, pp. 522–24.

and all she has done for him. Then she vents her rage upon him as he defends himself from her charges that he was an accomplice in her crimes. Jason pleads with her to restrain herself for the sake of their children. She begs him to flee with her; he pleads it is necessary to submit to Creon's power. She asks that her sons accompany her in exile; he declares his deep love for them, and refuses to part with them. Thereupon Medea conceives a shattering vengeance upon Jason—she will kill the children. She requests permission to bid them farewell. When he departs, she fumes with wrath and formulates her plans to the Nurse: she will send the children with a robe and diadem as gifts to Jason's bride, but first she will poison them with magic spells.

The Chorus comments on the fury of a wife spurned by her husband. The daring of men who leave the beaten path is criticized as being counter to the laws of nature. So, of those who sailed on the Argo many suffered disastrous ends, among them Tiphys, Orpheus, Hylas, Idmon, Meleager, and Mopsus. They pray that Jason may be spared.

ACT IV

The Nurse voices her fears of some coming disaster. She describes in elaborate detail Medea's resort to witchcraft—her concoction of a potent poison from serpent's venom, noxious herbs and other ingredients, such as unclean birds, a screech owl's heart, a vampire's vitals, and magic spells.

Medea appears, chanting her incantations and praying to diabolical supernatural forces for aid in her sorcery. In a savage frenzy she gashes her arm and lets the blood flow on the altar at which she is praying. Then she steeps in the potent drugs the robe and diadem to be sent as deadly gifts to Creusa, Jason's bride. She summons her sons and dispatches them abruptly to deliver the gifts.

The Chorus expresses horror at Medea's fury, and wishes she were already gone from Corinth.

ACT V

A messenger enters to report the catastrophe—the horrible deaths of Creusa and Creon, both consumed by the poisoned gifts, and the destruction of the palace by flames.

Medea, in a long soliloquy, gloats over the deaths of the king and the princess, and promises an even more horrible crime. She recalls in mad ecstasy all her past crimes. On the verge of murdering her sons, she wavers momentarily, touched by mother love. She embraces them, but hate speedily conquers love, and she submits to her desire for consummate vengeance upon Jason. She utters the macabre wish that she had had fourteen children . . . so that she might have even greater vengeance. A vision of the Furies [spirits who pursue murderers] and her brother's ghost appear to her. In wild frenzy she kills one of her sons on stage, and, as the sound of the outraged Corinthians coming to seize her is heard, she picks up the corpse and drags her surviving son inside her house.

Jason enters to seize Medea for punishment, and to burn her house to the ground. Suddenly Medea appears on the housetop with her two sons, boasting of her powers. Momentarily she is again seized by remorse, but at once feels a wild joy in her deed. She is not satisfied, because Jason did not view the killing of his son. He entreats her to spare the other boy, and offers himself as a victim in his place. Ruthlessly she slays the second son. Suddenly a chariot drawn by dragons appears to carry her off to safety. She flings the bodies down to him, as she is borne away.

A Modern Production of *Medea* Effectively Exploits Real Landscapes

Jan Kott

The characters in Euripides' *Medea* seem very realistic, even by today's standards. Yet in modern productions the play is usually staged much as the original was, in a stylistic rather than realistic manner, as exemplified by the chorus, a very formal stage and literary device. On at least one occasion, however, the play has been staged in such a way that it seemed eerily to merge with real life. This was the Greek traveling production that played in the town of Pescara (on Italy's eastern coast) in the early 1960s. The noted Polish-born scholar, Jan Kott (who has taught at Yale University and the University of California) witnessed this singular production and wrote about it in his book, *The Eating of the Gods*. In this moving excerpt, he tells how, in the outdoor theater, which was nestled on a ridge overlooking the sea, the settings seemed to grow out of the landscape, in many ways shedding their artificiality. And the characters, including the chorus members, seemed to merge, in looks and actions, with the local townspeople, whose provincial social traditions and problems were in many ways similar to those of the Greeks of long ago.

The Greek theatre [group] from the Piraeus [Athens's port town] had come with *Medea*. I went to see it in Pescara by a roundabout way, through Roccaraso and Palena, by-passing the Maiella ridge—the highest in the Abruzzi—from east and south.

Palena seemed to me the color of roasted coffee beans. The place was empty, as if burned out. Little towns in the

Excerpted from Jan Kott, *The Eating of the Gods*. Reprinted with permission from the author.

Abruzzi look like swallows' nests, or rather wasps' nests. Each is like a honeycomb plastered to a rock. In Umbria and in Provence, too, little towns seem molded together, with their buttresses, steep walls, their churches and castle which give one the impression of being stuck on to one another at the top. But in Umbria, villages and small towns ascend the slopes of gentle hills, sink into the green; hills become vineyards and olive groves. Here little towns are washed by rains and swept by winds. They belong wholly to this desert landscape, and at the same time bring some order into it and provide food for the imagination. Their beauty is austere, they have the protective colors of soil and stone—yellow and gray. Often they melt almost imperceptibly into a large empty rocky wall, or into heaps of yellow sand. It is these stony walls, big heaps of stones and sand, misty mountain tops and vast flat plains, shaped like huge plates, that combine to give the intriguing effect of a waste, a desert landscape. Men and animals are hardly ever seen in it. The little towns seem deserted. Only occasionally will one see donkeys slowly mounting the steep tracks, with their heavy loads of brush. They are led by old women, dressed in black, with cloths arranged flatly on their heads.

NATURE PROVIDES UNEXPECTED EFFECTS

The amphitheatre in Pescara is a new one, but it is situated outside the town, and there is nothing in its immediate vicinity. Only the sea is near. The night I was there, a cold wind was blowing from the sea, while hot air still came from the mountains. The stage area consisted of large stone steps. On top of them stood the Doric portico [porch] of Medea's house, with a huge closed door. Above the portico the moon was shining, quite low, cut in half. It was covered by clouds in the second half of the performance, almost immediately after Medea said she would murder her children and her rival.

Sometimes natural scenery gives unexpected effects, as when all of a sudden the sky or birds start playing their part. Once I saw *Hamlet* performed in the courtyard of Elsinore Castle [in Denmark, where the play is set]. During the first great soliloquy some gulls flew just above Hamlet's head, and a couple of them suddenly squatted at his feet.

In the enclosed theatre there is no room for the Chorus, even when the designer extends the forestage halfway through the front rows. The entry of the Chorus is artificial.

One does not know whether to keep it there, or to let it come on and off the stage every time. In every performance of Greek tragedies that I had seen, the Chorus had always been a disguised ballet. But the Chorus in Sophocles and Euripides is not a ballet interlude, or an intellectual commentary. It is not external or added on to the tragedy; it does not need any justification. The Chorus is simply the people. Fourteen young women stopped on the stone steps. They had entered the way peasant women do, like the girls in Pescocostanzo when they assemble in the evening by the fountain in the town square. . . .

THE NIGHT WAS REAL

I do not know what impression *Medea* makes in the marble amphitheatre of Greece. Perhaps it seems monumental and remote. Here in Pescara, from the very first scene, Medea and the Chorus of young women seemed to belong to the soil, the landscape. Medea was in buskins, I suppose because the part was played by a tiny actress. She was an ordinary Medea, humanly unhappy and humanly vindictive; she was like those peasant women, stiff and erect under the fifty-pound loads on their heads, tired but still full of dignity. There was something about her too, of that night, when the sea blew cold wind alternately with the stifling hot wind from the Maiella ridge.

The action of Euripides' *Medea* lasts from the early morning until late in the night. But here the real time and the time of performance were the same. A few hours of such a night were enough to accomplish mad deeds that would seem impossible in the daytime. Daylight would disperse madness like the mists . . . in the mornings.

Not only time was condensed. The unity of place seemed just as natural, there was nothing of contrived poetics about it. I still remember my shock on my first visit to Rome that the Forum Romanum was so small. Just a few hundred steps from the Capitol and the Tarpeian Rock to the Arch to Titus. . . . Kings, patricians and plebeians, republicans; all the tribunes and all the consuls, the Ides of March, Nero and Caligula—that square between two hills was enough to provide the setting for almost the entire history of Rome. Just one setting. The Acropolis is even smaller than the Roman Forum. . . .

On the little square in front of Medea's house one could hear the groans of Glauca being burned alive. In the last

scene Jason ran in out of breath; he had run up the hundred
steps from the royal palace. Earlier still, Aegeus had appeared: he had come directly from a small harbor where he
had left his boat. That fishing harbor could almost be seen
from Medea's house. In nearly every tragedy, a ship is waiting in the harbor with sails set. The ship means an escape.
But the true heroes are shut in the palace. The palace is both
prison and asylum. They cannot go away. If they could go
away, there would be no tragedy. Only their confidants are
free to go. . . .

To me, the unity of place in an indoor theatre always
seemed artificial. Here, however, everything is close at hand.
In the *Medea* at Pescara, night was really night, stone steps
were stone steps, the nearby sea was a nearby sea. . . .

GOD HAS NOT CHANGED

Medea does not address the gods. They do not exist for her,
just as the world does not exist, as her children do not exist.
For her, they are Jason's children. More than that, they are
Jason himself. She kills them not only to revenge herself on
him but because she cannot kill Jason; she kills Jason in
them. But actually even Jason does not exist for Medea. Only
she exists; she and her defeat. She cannot even for a moment
talk or think about anything else. She is locked within herself with her misfortune, as if inside an egg. Medea's mad
monomania [absorption with one's self] is undoubtedly a
Euripidean discovery. Monomania singles Medea out, sepa-
rates and cuts her off from the real world. Through her
monomania Medea is alone. Heroes of tragedy have to be
alone.

But the Chorus of women is of this world. They have come
from the village, from the small harbor which is also a village. They have come to commiserate with Medea. She has
been deserted by her husband; now they want to take her
sons away. In its first odes the Chorus complains of the injustice of the human lot and says that bitter is the life of a girl
who remains unmarried, and bitter the life of a woman who
marries. The women are on Medea's side and will remain so
to the end. But gradually they become more and more terri-
fied, not only by Medea's designs but by the ordeal sent her
by the gods. The women's gestures become more and more
liturgical. They fall on their knees, begin to beg for mercy
and pity, but not for themselves. They beg the god for mercy

who takes revenge on Medea, Jason, Creon; who takes vengeance on children for parents' misdeeds, and on grandchildren for those of their grandparents.

It suddenly seemed to me that the women, who went to the top of the stairs to the shut door of Medea's house, began to recite the litany to the Virgin [Mary], or to the Heart of Jesus. They were praying, and their prayer was one long moan.

A few days earlier, on the way back from my evening stroll, on the stone steps in front of the collegiate church of Santa Maria del Colle, I had noticed a group of women, dressed in black, reciting a litany. It had been the same kind of moaning that I heard then. The words "have mercy on us" had been shouted almost like a cry of despair. The door of Santa Maria del Colle remained closed. God had literally locked himself in.

The day after the performance of *Medea*, I went to the old fishing harbor in Pescara. In the square, by the entrance to a small house, stood a tall column with the statue of the Virgin. The column and the statue were ugly. They had been erected between the two world wars. On the column was the inscription: "Mary, Queen of Heaven, Mary who rules the thunder, do not kill the sons of Pescara." For the last two weeks it had been raining heavily. . . . The harvest had been soaked; hay could not be brought in. Yesterday, and the day before, bells rang in all the churches. . . . They rang for two hours, from seven to eight in the morning and from three to four in the afternoon: seven bells of the splendidly gilded fourteenth-century Santa Maria del Colle; two shrill little bells of the new church on the rock—San Antonio Abate, and—loudest of all—four bells of the dei Fratri convent, with their monotonous and ominous sound. They had rung so that God would take pity and avert the calamity of rain. . . . Today they rang again; they will ring tomorrow and the day after tomorrow.

The persistent, mournful, fierce ringing of bells might end the Greek tragedy with which the Greek theatre from Piraeus came to Pescara. The bells . . . have been ringing to appease the same god who punished Medea and the family of Jason. For it is men who are always guilty; never God. God has not changed here for three thousand years.

The Play's Success Now Rests on the Actress in the Title Role

Karelisa V. Hartigan

Modern American productions of *Medea* have always been dominated by the actresses playing the title role. This is partly because of the prominent
place actors and actresses play in American culture.
It is also because the role, as written, is large, highly
theatrical, and a supreme challenge for any actress
to assail believably and successfully. Thus, it tends
to attract great actresses with larger-than-life repu-
tations and/or personalities. As Karelisa V. Hartigan,
a professor of Classics at the University of Florida,
explains here, each new major stage presentation of
Medea has come to rest "upon the power of an exceptional actress." She gives several examples, including the most renowned and acclaimed Medea of
the twentieth century—English actress Judith Anderson, who won a Tony Award for her performance
in 1947. (The version in which Anderson became famous was an adaptation of Euripides' original by
American poet Robinson Jeffers, who died in 1962.)
Among the other productions of the play Hartigan
discusses are those starring American actress Zoe
Caldwell (who won the Tony for her Medea in 1982)
and English actress Diana Rigg (who won the Tony
for her Medea in 1994).

When Robinson Jeffers determined to write his new version
of Euripides' play of 431 B.C., he took his cue, perhaps, from
French playwrights of that time who composed a drama for
a specific actress. Thus he rewrote Euripides' *Medea*, which
opened in October of 1947, for his favorite leading lady, Judith Anderson. Over the next three years Miss Anderson

Excerpted from Karelisa V. Hartigan, *Greek Tragedy on the American Stage.* Copyright
© 1995 by Karelisa V. Hartigan. Reprinted with permission from Greenwood Publishing Group, Inc., Westport, CT.

would play the barbarian princess from Colchis, wronged by
the politically eager Jason, for 214 performances. She toured
worldwide with Jeffers' play, and each time she took the
stage, critics and audiences alike hailed her performance.
Anderson's interpretation of Medea has dominated American theater history, but it should be noted that while Judith
Anderson stands at the center, she shares the limelight with
two other fine actresses who brought the role alive, Margaret Anglin in the 1920s and Zoe Caldwell in the 1980s.

Medea has remained one of the most popular plays from
antiquity to be brought to the modern American stage. The
desire to produce this one of Euripides' dramas must rest,
ultimately, on its theatricality and the strong character of
Medea herself: her great scenes are a challenge for any actress. Its appeal is somewhat mysterious, however, for any
character analysis of Medea reveals some very troubling
ideas: we are prepared to sympathize with the woman
scorned, but not ready to condone her violent deed; it is one
thing to applaud revenge taken upon the deserting husband,
but quite another to sanction a mother's deliberate slaughter
of her own children. . . .

What are we to make of Medea, this foreign woman re-
moved to Greek soil and there abandoned? Some scholars
have suggested that Euripides intended her to be a paradigm
[model] warning against women in general, foreign women
in particular. Others have taken her at face value and argued
that she is in the right because Jason broke his oath to her,
and thus she illustrates the dangers that follow those who do
so. Another view removes her from the mortal realm alto-
gether; as the granddaughter of the sun, her access to magical powers exonerates her of blame: she acts as does any
Greek deity when wronged. This view gathers strength from
the play's ending, when Helios' chariot comes and whisks
her away to safety, a mother still stained from the blood of
her children. All of these interpretations have some validity.

Whatever the Greek view may have been, modern producers want the audience to side with Medea, while actresses find in her strong character a role to covet. Few great
women of the stage can resist the opportunity to proclaim
Medea's famous lines (250–251): "I would rather stand forth
in battle three times than once to bear a single child." Thus
the performance history of *Medea* reveals that great actresses in the title role have dominated the interpretation of

the play on the twentieth-century American stage. This was true in the 1920s, the 1950s, and the 1980s; that the play's attraction rests on a leading actress is equally true in the 1990s, for Diana Rigg's interpretation in 1994 earned her international recognition: the 1994 Tony Award went to an actress bringing to life a play nearly 2,500 years old.

TWO EARLY AMERICAN PRODUCTIONS

One of the earliest [modern American] interpretations of Medea was that given by Margaret Anglin at Carnegie Hall in February 1918. As Anglin won acclaim for her portrayal of Electra during the same billing, so she did for her performance in *Medea.* "The barbaric heroine of Euripides rendered with true classic intensity and fire," headlines the *New York Times* (21 February 1918) review. While in his plot summary the (anonymous) reviewer shows some sympathy for Jason—"poor man, her husband and at once the cause of her fury and the chief object of it"—he admits that it is to Medea that Euripides directs his (and our) concern:

> [She is] a very moving figure—splendid, too, caught as she is in a vortex of elemental feminine passions, richly colored by her barbaric soul. . . . She has all the primitive woman's love for her children, yet . . . she kills them both. . . . [Thus does she] leave Jason without bride, kingdom or child.

The role itself permitted Anglin to display her talents in portraying two very different sides of the heroine. While the reviewer concedes that there were perhaps depths to Medea's character that the young actress could not reach, he admits that she was "consummate" both in tenderness toward her children and violence in her rage. *Theatre Magazine's* reviewer Mr. Hornblow agreed:

> Most lavish praise [should] be paid to Miss Anglin for the vividly varied reading she gave of the daughter of the Barbarian queen. . . . As a declamatory *tour de force* it was remarkable, aided by pantomimic intelligence and plastic grace that gave its varying words and eloquence tremendous [power] in its onrushing sweep of tragic significance. . . .

Two years later, however, the reviewers were somewhat less tolerant of the ancient Greek classic. [Producer-director] Maurice Browne's Little Theatre troupe came east from Chicago to play *Medea* at the Garrick and earned less glowing comments. Several reviewers were distressed as much by the text as by the acting; this time, indeed, Hornblow himself (*Theatre Magazine*, 20 May 1920) complained that it was "a fearful strain to sit still for two hours" of Euripides. But while this critic had only praise for Maurice Browne's "artistic intelligence" and "physical grasp of stage opportunities," others were impressed more with Browne's *intent* than his *result*: the former was admirable, but the latter less successful; the production was artistic but not vital.

Ellen Van Volkenburg did not rival Margaret Anglin in her portrayal of the wronged queen. . . . J. Ranken Towse (*New York Evening Post,* 23 March 1920) asserted she lacked the "skill, pathos and passion" of Anglin. The 1918 performance by Margaret Anglin had become the standard by which to judge any actress playing the title role. . . .

JUDITH ANDERSON'S MEDEA

The version of *Medea* most frequently staged is not Euripides' "original" but the free adaptation Robinson Jeffers wrote for Judith Anderson. The 1947 program note describes the play as "a tragedy in two acts about the vengeance of a woman scorned by her ambitious husband." *Medea* opened with Jason played by John Gielgud, who also directed the show; he was eventually replaced by Dennis King. The show was revived for a limited run (sixteen performances) at the New York City Center in May 1949, at which time Henry Brandon played Jason to Anderson's Medea.

"If Medea does not entirely understand every aspect of her whirling character, she would do well to consult Judith Anderson. For Miss Anderson understands the character more thoroughly than Medea, Euripides, or the scholars, and it would be useless now for anyone else to attempt the part." So does Brooks Atkinson begin his review (*New York Times,* 21 October 1947) of the Jeffers/Anderson show. His praise extended to the entire performance: John Gielgud's Jason is described as "lucid [and] solemn"; Albert Hecht [the actor who played Creon], he claims, "has the commanding voice and the imperiousness of a working monarch." The chorus, comprised of just three women, was well directed by Gielgud; indeed, all of the acting, according to Atkinson, was "innocent of the stuffiness peculiar to most classical productions." He closes his review with further praise of Judith Anderson: "She has freed Medea from all the old traditions as if the character had just been created. Perhaps that is exactly what has happened. Perhaps Medea was never fully created until Miss Anderson breathed immortal fire into it last evening."

Atkinson was so struck with Anderson's performance in Jeffers' *Medea* that a few days later (26 October 1947) he wrote a two-column piece on the play. Here he had the opportunity not only to praise Anderson's acting abundantly, but also to write about Greek culture. . . .

Atkinson dares to break away from the common assumption that the civilization of ancient Athens was innocent of any wrongs. It is to Euripides' credit, he asserts, that he did not "conform to the accepted patterns." Thus in *Medea* he portrayed the marriage of a Greek to a foreigner—"still an abomination in cultures that are pure and intolerant" and "faced honestly the injustice that a Greek man had done a foreign woman." Such attitudes would eventually earn the playwright exile to Macedonia, since the Creons of ancient Athens "felt safer when he was out of the way."

In the final sections of his article Atkinson deals with Jeffers' sensible and dramatic updating of Euripides' text and Gielgud's directing. The only cavil he made was against the decision to tame Medea's murder of her two sons. Such a drama as *Medea*, he states, "needs that climax of inhuman horror to complete the design," and such a great actress as Anderson does "not boggle at violence." Gifted with such praise, Judith Anderson in the title role of Jeffers' *Medea* went on her extensive tour of the United States and Europe. . . .

THE TORCH PASSES TO ZOE CALDWELL

In the spring of 1982, Judith Anderson returned to the American stage in *Medea*, but this time as the Nurse, playing the servant to Zoe Caldwell's Medea. Some critics thought that even in the lesser role she still dominated the performance; they found Caldwell's acting much weaker than Anderson's had been in the lead role. Douglas Watt (*Daily News*, 3 May 1982) proclaimed, "Judith Anderson [as the Nurse] is the one moving thing about the revival [of Jeffers' *Medea*]. . . . Even in repose Anderson, whose electrifying Medea is still vivid in the memory, commands our attention."

But Watt was in the minority. Most critics had only praise for the interpretation given the role by Zoe Caldwell. Continuities abounded: Ben Edwards, who designed the 1947 production, also staged that of 1982, and he maintained the classic concepts that had worked forty years earlier. Thus the young actress had to re-create Medea in the setting her elder supporting actress had made famous. To the majority of

New York critics her attempt was eminently successful.

Frank Rich, writing in the *New York Times* (3 May 1982), asserts that Zoe Caldwell "brought her special flame" to the revival. Her "intense psychological realism" brought her audience into "the thunderclap of Euripides' tragedy," leading them to believe in her warped logic. Her physical appearance set her off from those around her: she looked the part, states Rich, as well as interpreting it. He praises her wit, her sexuality, and her speech. While Rich cannot acclaim the entire production, he finally hails the play as powerful and exciting. He is echoed by John Beaufort of the *Christian Science Monitor* (6 May 1982), who, in a review titled "Zoe Caldwell's *Medea*, a Theatrical Mountaintop," accords accolades to the entire show. Caldwell, he states, "scales the histrionic heights" in the title role. She portrayed guile, cunning, deep hurt, and sorrow as she commanded "the spectator's understanding of this jealousy-maddened creature." While his approval of Judith Anderson's performance as the Nurse was expected, Beaufort even liked Michael Ryan's Jason: "the middle-aged power-conscious Jason is a plausible climber, the one-time varsity hero now angling for a place in the executive suite." Setting, direction, music—all moved this member of the audience: "Count *Medea* a theatrical event in the grand tradition. In other words, a summit." The critic takes time to discuss Greek drama as well.

Although one of the most popular plays from the alien world of Greek tragedy, *Medea* presents special problems for a latter-day audience. Oedipus, after all, didn't realize that he was committing patricide and, ultimately, incest. However, given her extreme emotional disarray, Medea knows what she is doing at every step. . . . Was Medea ignoble and base or was she rather a primitive (a "barbarian" as she scornfully proclaims), a woman totally ruled by extremes of passion? . . . The bottom line of Medea's motivation is reached in her explanation to [the] distraught father: "I have done it: because I loathed you more than I loved them.". . .

The Caldwell-Anderson *Medea* had come to New York from its opening at the Kennedy Center in Washington, DC. There, too, the theater critics found superlatives in order. Joseph McLellan of the *Washington Post* (12 March 1982), who gives high praise to the leading actresses, chose an unusual way to describe Euripides' play. Beginning by suggesting that "Greek tragedy is not everybody's cup of retsina, but *Medea* is one of the few exceptions to the rule that this art is box-office poison.". . .

The Washington critics focused particularly on the dramatic tradition that the two actresses were creating in this new production, a passing on of the torch of a great role from one leading lady to another. There was an additional unusual aspect to this *Medea*. The 1982 production was directed by Robert Whitehead, Zoe Caldwell's husband, who had produced the 1947 version. During that run, however, Whitehead and Anderson had had a falling out, and the two had not communicated for nearly thirty years.

Then in 1979 Anderson, seeking funding for the restoration of Jeffers' home, Tor House, in Carmel, California, considered the possibility of staging his most famous play again. She knew Caldwell's ability and thought she would be right for the part. Anderson indirectly contacted Whitehead about the script, then invited him and Caldwell to meet with her, and finally persuaded them to mount the show. Thus it was through Judith Anderson's vision that, once again, Jeffers' *Medea* was brought to critical acclaim. While Anderson's portrayal of the Nurse was praised, she herself willingly accorded the top laurels to Caldwell, whose acting "completed the circle." Responding in an interview about the production, Judith Anderson said, "It's a great role, all right, and it was written for me. Once it was mine. Now it belongs to Zoe.". . .

MEDEAS OF THE 1990s

In the winter of 1991, the Guthrie Theater mounted a performance of Euripides' *Medea*. The text was that of the Athenian playwright in a translation by Philip Vellacott. This was the first Greek show directed by [director] Garland Wright, an undertaking he claimed to approach with fear, but his venture was defined by Mike Steele (*Minneapolis Star and Tribune*, 14 January 1991) as a "first-rate merging of archaic grandeur and contemporary sensibilities." Its grandeur and power lay in the acting of Brenda Wehle as Medea, and in that of the three women of the chorus, Isabell Monk, Jacqueline Kim, and Sally Wingert.

At first Wehle felt some trepidation about playing the title role in this play. Wright thought it important that Medea be played by a mother, but Wehle had to come to terms with a woman who would slay her own children. In an interview with Mike Steele in the *Minneapolis Star and Tribune* (11 January 1991) Wehle spoke about her relationship with the play's main character. To experience Medea's passion, she stated, "was scary, no fun at all." But as she developed the character, she came to understand drama itself as a cleansing ritual, one that allowed people to admit their darkest fears and not carry them out. At last she achieved a balance between her anger and her sadness, all the while amazed at Euripides' understanding of Medea.

The critics acclaimed Brenda Wehle's rendition of the barbarian princess. They described her performance as powerful, full of energy, one that brought to life the grief and rage that would ultimately compel her terrible deed of revenge. Those upon whom she vented that anger, however, the men of the play, were uniformly described as weak actors, cold, flat, lacking in both vitality and intensity. The Guthrie *Medea* was ranked a success through the vibrant interpretation given by the women of the cast.

Zoe Caldwell won a Tony Award in 1982 for her portrayal of the title role in the Euripides /Jeffers play, as had Judith Anderson in 1947. The award was granted to an actress in the ancient play once again in 1994. Diana Rigg, who first created the role in London, brought life to Euripides' text (in a new translation by Alistair Elliot) on the New York stage, and most printed reviews pointed out her talent. Edwin Wilson, theater critic of the *Wall Street Journal*, hailed Rigg's "incredible vocal range," "her presence and bearing." In his 13 April 1994 review he continues: "Ms. Rigg moves like quicksilver from one emotion to another but always with an unmistakable resolve. Her Medea is not a mindless barbarian but rather someone who knows exactly what she is doing . . . [she] moves relentlessly toward her goal. This makes the outcome that much more awesome and appalling."

Even the critics who were less fulsome in their praise termed the performance a "theatrical event" and Rigg's interpretation regal, if overly civilized; Vincent Canby (*New York Times*, 17 April 1994) complained that by her costume this Medea looked less like a barbarian than "the fashion plate of Corinth." William A. Henry III, writing for *Time* (25 April 1994). . . hailed the final tableau as making the competent production unforgettable. In the surprising last scene, the bronze wall toppled to reveal Diana Rigg apparently already at sea. Hunched during her period of rage and oppression, she stands proud as a ship's figurehead, clouds streaming past, golden light burnishing her. Then she turns and looks back, toward the scene of her unrepented misdeeds and, surely, toward an audience agape at the beauty and power of this finale.

Rigg's Medea was not at sea, but airborne, for as the legend tells us, her grandfather Helios, the sun god, had sent his chariot to carry her to Athens. The vision of her triumphant flight persists and offers a fitting closure to this show's production history, a show which in each revival has rested upon the power of an exceptional actress.

A Film Version Depicts Medea's Barbarous Background

Jon Solomon

Perhaps the most difficult aspect of the story of *Medea* for audiences, both ancient and modern, to accept is the title character's savage murder of her own children. To say, simply, that she has been driven to such an extreme act by Jason's cruelty is not enough to make such an act by a mother believable. For ancient Greek audiences at least, there was the realization that in the myths about Jason and Medea she comes from a non-Greek and therefore less civilized land (Colchis, on the shores of the Black Sea); and this seems partially to explain why she could stoop to such seeming barbarity. Still, when audiences watch the play, they only *hear* about Medea's background. They do not witness it first-hand, and so they must use their imaginations to visualize the less-than-civilized society that produced her. This is the sort of problem that the artistic medium of film excels at solving. In 1970, Italian director Pier Paolo Pasolini filmed Euripides' *Medea* and boldly confronted the issue of her barbarous personality. As classical scholar and film critic Jon Solomon explains in this excerpt from his fascinating book chronicling movies about the ancient world, Pasolini opens his film in Colchis. By showing in graphic detail human sacrifice and other bloody aspects of that culture, the filmmaker helps the audience to understand Medea in terms of her background and thereby provides a believable explanation for her later acts of murder and infanticide.

This film includes a prologue that explains the mythological background to the Euripidean drama. In this case, Pasolini reconstructs the voyage of the Argo, with its heroes Jason,

Excerpted from Jon Solomon, *The Ancient World in the Cinema*. Reprinted with permission from the author.

Orpheus, Castor, and Pollux (Polydeuces), from Greece to the Eastern land of Colchis. But the vast majority of footage concentrates not on the heroic voyage itself, which for Pasolini is made on a large raft and without incident, but on life in Colchis. Colchis, as Euripides describes it, was a barbaric, uncivilized land at the end of the Greek world. Pasolini takes this information and then reenacts the anthropological and spiritual rituals, particular vegetation rituals, that made such a prehistoric (or metahistorical) world so innocently savage. These vegetation rituals involve *sparagmos*, or tearing apart of sacrificial humans, scattering their limbs among the crops, and wetting the fields with their blood. The major idea underlying this ritual is resurrection—that the dead sacrificial victim will rise again with healthy crops in the following harvest.

DEATH, BLOOD, AND SACRIFICE ARE HER LIFE

The reenacting and filming of such a bloody ritual, especially with the visual detail and starkness so often associated with Pasolini, gives *Medea* its unique beginning, but the desired effect is not really the blood and anthropological correctitude. It is the ritualistic essence of the "barbaric" culture of which Medea herself is a vital part, a priestess, in fact, and the granddaughter of the Sun God. Pasolini makes it clear that this ritual is as real and important to Medea as the sophisticated culture of Greece is to Jason (and Euripides). Medea can therefore be understood only in terms of her culture. For her to kill her two children (by Jason) is for her to react naturally. Death, blood, and sacrifice are her life, hope, and safety. Early in the film, when Jason coldly steals the Golden Fleece from her native Colchis, he is in a sense robbing her of this ritualistic life-line. She now submits herself to Jason and his Hellenic culture. But when Jason (Olympic high-jumper Giuseppe Gentili) leaves her for the Corinthian princess Glauce, Medea then returns to her ritualistic origins; and Pasolini makes this known by Medea's praying to her divine solar grandfather. The camera boldly blears the hazy ball of fiery sun rising over the still, ashen, morning sea; and prepared by the geophysical and animistic setting in the early sequences of the film, this sun truly seems to be a god and Medea's grandfather. Pasolini has reached beyond the historic barriers of Greek mythology and recaptured the prehistoric animism that primitive man found so productive. By doing so he enabled himself to give a reasonable explanation for Medea's calculated slaughter of her babes.

THE CIVILIZED RITUALS OF CORINTH

To strengthen visually this cinematic presentation of prehistoric animistic worship, Pasolini shot the Colchis sequences in the unique valley of Göreme in central Turkey. Here majestic rock cones jut seventy-five feet into the sky, and dark chapels hollowed out from their insides provide the perfectly primitive and sacred housing for the Golden Fleece and its priests. The Fleece itself does not glitter or change color as in Ray Harryhausen's *Jason and the Argonauts*; it is instead a bland, unremarkably yellowish fleece with which Pasolini implies that marvelous rumors from distant Eastern Islands may not be as wondrous as they are supposed to be. Since the "magic" of the Colchian Golden Fleece derived only from its primitive ritualistic importance, to Pasolini's civilized Jason the Fleece would not seem magical at all.

The vegetation ritual that opens the film graphically depicts the death of the young male victim, the scattering of his limbs, and the spreading of his blood over the nearby crops. Piero Tosi's costumes, furs, bells, and strangely bulky jewelry present even more oddities to the sequence. The Persian santur music and close-harmonied Balkan choral singing surrounds the visual aspects of the sequence with an aura of plaintive provocation. In great contrast are the scenes of Greek Corinth. Here Pasolini (like Euripides) tries visually to suggest the "civilized rituals" of more modern, Western society, and so the palace of King Creon (Massimo Girotti in still another ancient role) becomes the cathedral and famed baptistry of Pisa; its white marble and verdant malls alone remind us that the rocky moonscape of Göreme and Colchis belong to a different civilization. A man of subtleties and symbolism, Pasolini calmly includes several boys eating juicy red watermelons on the cathedral (palace) steps; this very brief tableau reflects the ironic difference between the bloody red, human vegetation victim in Colchis and juicy red watermelons in Corinth (though this, like all Pasolini's visual symbols, carries many different interpretations).

Pasolini provides more contrast at the death of Glauce. Medea, just as in Euripides' play, sends her two boys to Princess Glauce with a wedding gift; she wants to show

Glauce that there are no hard feelings between the two women in Jason's life, so she says. When Glauce puts on Medea's magical raiments, she bursts into flames and runs out of the palace. Glauce leaps from the walls of the palace to her death. Such action was not shown on the Athenian stage; it was, as usual, described in the "messenger speech." But Pasolini shows it twice, once as dreamed by Medea, and once as it actually happened. Medea's dream is introduced merely by a double-exposed shot of Göreme's cones and the haunting santur music, so haunting are these, our visual and aural memories of Colchis. The two death sequences have their differences, however, because Pasolini is describing, on purely visual terms, the differences between reality and mental conception. The intellectual stimulation from Glauce's death scenes grows even more intense when Pasolini shoots the interior of the palace of Corinth in Pisa, but the exterior walls (from which Glauce leaps) at the ramparts of Aleppo, Syria.

A TRULY MYTHOLOGICAL PERFORMANCE

To effect the awesome barbarity and savage vengeance in the story, Pasolini needed a Medea who could dominate the screen and seem perfectly natural in this barbaric role. She had to be an actress of priestly, royal, aristocratic manner, capable of loving a man and two children, yet also capable of killing the children to spite him. Maria Callas is perfect. Without singing a note, other than humming a lullaby to one son just before his death, Callas completely dominates the screen whenever she appears. Her strong cheeks and proud nose peer from under a black mantle; she seems relaxed during the vegetation rites and just as relaxed during the execution of her sons, and yet her agony is somehow apparent. A truly mythological performance, Maria Callas displays the grandeur, sorcery, evil, and power that have always been associated with Medea, yet all this with the slightest touch of mortal, womanly emotion. Mother, lover, daughter and sister, by the film's end Medea has destroyed all the males in her life, and she knows it.

APPENDIX: ORIGINS AND DEVELOPMENT OF GREEK DRAMA AND THEATER

Greek drama and theater developed with relative suddenness and enjoyed their greatest flowering in Athens in the brief period spanning the late sixth through late fifth centuries B.C. Although the exact origins of these literary and visual arts are and will likely always remain uncertain, scholars have managed to piece together a likely scenario for their inception. At least by the eighth century B.C., the Greeks had developed elaborate rituals attending worship of the fertility god Dionysus, including a kind of poetry and ceremony called the dithyramb. This special form of verse, which the worshipers sang and danced to, eventually became the chief highlight of the religious festivals dedicated to the god. Apparently the dithyramb told the story of Dionysus's life and adventures, as set down in various myths the Greeks had inherited from earlier times.

As time went on, the dithyrambic ceremony expanded to include other gods, as well as human heroes, and took on increasingly dramatic form. A priest and a selected group of worshipers stood in front of the rest of the congregation and, to the accompaniment of flutes, cymbals, and other instruments, enacted a god's or hero's story through song and dance. In a way, then, the priest and his assistants were the first performers and the rest of the congregation their audience. Another advance occurred when priests began elaborating on and offering their own versions of the accepted story lines; this made them, in a sense, the first playwrights. In fact, this is exactly the way Aristotle thought drama originated. Tragedy (the first form drama took), he said,

> certainly began in improvisations [spontaneous creations]... originating with the authors of the dithyramb... which still survive... in many of our cities. And its advance [evolution into the art of drama] after that was little by little, through their improving on whatever they had before them at each stage.[1]

Another piece of evidence supporting this scenario for tragedy's origins is that the dithyramb was also called "goat-song" because some of those involved in the ceremony dressed as satyrs (creatures part-man and part-animal, usually a goat or horse). The term "tragedy" (*tragoidia*) most likely developed from the Greek words *tragos,* meaning goat, and *odi,* meaning song.

Another important source for drama was epic poetry, especially the epics of Homer. At first, bards like Homer merely stood before an audience (probably mainly aristocrats initially) and recited these tales. In time, however, such recitations became more formal and attached to religious festivals. An important turning point came in 566 B.C. when the Athenians instituted Homeric recitation contests—the *rhapsodia.* (The performers were known as *rhapsodes.*)

THE FIRST THEATRICAL COMPETITIONS

Not long afterward, perhaps about the year 534 B.C., Athens instituted a large-scale annual religious festival—the City Dionysia—in Dionysus's honor. The festival featured a dramatic competition involving both formal dithyramb and *rhapsodia.* The contest's first winner was a poet named Thespis, who is credited with transforming these traditional presentations into the first example of what later came to be recognized as a theatrical play, part of a new art form called tragedy. Thespis's play utilized most of the standard elements of the dithyramb and *rhapsodia* but featured some important innovations. One was the addition of a chorus to the *rhapsodia.* Evidently, the chorus members recited in unison some of the lines and also commented on the events of the story to heighten the dramatic effect. Thespis's other novel idea was to impersonate, rather than just tell about, the story's heroes. In detaching himself from the chorus and playing a character, he became the world's first actor.

In a sense, then, Thespis created the formal art form of theater almost overnight. In setting up regular interplay between actor and chorus, he introduced the basic theatrical convention of dialogue; he also experimented with ways of disguising himself so that he could portray different characters in the same dramatic piece. He eventually decided to don a series of masks, which became another standard convention of Greek theater. In addition, Thespis apparently helped to define the role of the audience. By enlarging the dithyramb into a piece of art and entertainment, he transformed the congregation into a true theater audience. (For these innovations, Thespis became a theater immortal; actors are still called "thespians" in his honor.)

A number of talented and ambitious writer-actor-managers soon entered the new art form Thespis had introduced and competed with him in the City Dionysia. Among these pioneers were Choerilus, who wrote some 160 plays and won the great dramatic competition thirteen times; and Pratinas, who wrote perhaps eighteen tragedies. For subjects, these men relied mainly on the standard Greek myths, as well as on the tales in the *Iliad* and other epics (most of which are now lost). On occasion, they also depicted important recent historical events. The popular playwright Phrynichus, for instance, made a stir at the City Dionysia around 492 B.C. for his play *The Fall of Miletus,* about the Persian capture of that prosperous Ionian Greek city. According to the fifth-century B.C. Greek historian Herodotus, the play was so moving that the audience burst into tears.

Unfortunately, all of the plays of these early theater giants are lost. However, the survival of a few fragments, as well as descriptions of the plays by later writers, provide a rough idea of how they appeared in performance. A single actor engaged in dialogue with the chorus leader while the other chorus members reacted to the conversation with elegant patterned gestures; between "scenes," the chorus danced and sang choral odes (songs) that related to the action of the story.

Such performances became increasingly elaborate and dramatic, and the City Dionysia festival accordingly developed into a major holiday attraction that the populace eagerly awaited each year. Covering several days at the end of March, the festival was open to all Greeks; that is, people from other city-states could attend or enter plays in the competition. However, the competition itself, including all play production, remained an Athenian monopoly for a long time to come. Not surprisingly then, the Athenian government wisely took advantage of the celebration as a showcase for the city's growing wealth and cultural achievements. To this end, the state financed the theater building and its maintenance, paid fees to the actors (and possibly the playwrights), and also provided the prizes for the dramatic contests. All other expenses of play production, including costumes, sets, musicians, and the training of the choruses, were the responsibility of the backers, the *choregoi,* well-to-do citizens whom the state called on to help support the festival. These men were chosen by lot (random drawing) each year and each *choregus* was assigned to a specific playwright.

How the Plays Were Presented

As for the duties of the playwrights themselves, in addition to writing the plays they usually acted in them, trained the choruses, composed the music, choreographed the dances, and supervised all other aspects of production. In fact, they were so involved in instructing others that at the time they were known as *didaskaliai,* meaning teachers. Typically, rehearsals lasted for months and continued right up until the opening of the festival.

On the first day of the competition, the playwrights, their *choregoi* and choruses, along with important public officials, took part in a stately procession that wound its way through the city streets. The colorful parade ended up in the Theater of Dionysus (near the southeastern foot of the Acropolis), which sat about 14,000 spectators. After the procession entered the theater, the public sacrifice of a bull to Dionysus took place. Then the competitions started with the dithyrambic contests, a gesture to tradition. Finally, in the days that followed, each of three playwrights presented three tragedies. (Tragedy was still the main dramatic form, as comedy was not yet well developed or popular; when comedies eventually began to be performed at the City Dionysia in 501 B.C., they took place at night, after day-long presentations of tragedy.)

Probably the festival's most eagerly awaited moment was the awards ceremony, in many ways an ancient counterpart to today's Oscar night. The winners were chosen by a panel of ten judges, and the prizes consisted of crowns of ivy, which were awarded to the *choregoi* rather than to the playwrights. The victors also received lavish praise, so it is certain that one of the main incentives for a backer was the knowledge that winning would greatly increase his prestige in the community.

The exact criteria the judges used to choose the victors of the festival competitions are unknown. Likewise, the precise look of the plays during Greek drama's golden age in the mid-to-late fifth century B.C. are uncertain. However, scenes painted on vases and cups, various ancient literary descriptions, and other evidence provide a general idea. The actors wore elaborate masks and both white and brightly-colored costumes; they also used props, as modern actors do, although the Greeks used them more sparingly. The most common props were chariots, couches, statues of gods, shields and swords, and biers to display dead bodies.

The settings, on the other hand, were left mostly to the audience's imagination. In the fifth and fourth centuries B.C., as a rule the action of the plays took place outdoors, in front of a house, palace, temple, or other familiar structure. The scene building (*skene*) that stood behind the actors, redecorated appropriately by the playwright-producer, represented the fronts of these buildings. Interiors could not be shown, and there is no solid evidence for the use of movable painted scenery like that in modern theaters.

As time went on, Greek theatrical producers introduced various mechanical devices to enhance both setting and atmosphere. Perhaps the most common was the *eccyclema*, or "tableau machine." Violent acts were almost always committed "indoors," and therefore offstage and out of sight, and the audience learned about them secondhand from messengers or other characters. Sometimes, however, to achieve shock value, a doorway in the *skene* would open and stagehands would push out the *eccyclema*, a movable platform on rollers. On the platform, frozen in a dramatic, posed tableau, would be both the murderer and the victim, usually depicted in the seconds immediately following the crime.

Other mechanical devices included a "lightning machine" (*keraunoskopeion*); "thunder machine" (*bronteion*); and the *machina* (the source of the word machine), a crane with a mechanical arm used to "fly" an actor playing a god or hero through the air above the stage. Over the years, playwrights tended to overuse the *machina* to show gods arriving in the finale to resolve the story's conflicts in a simple, neat way. Thus, the term *deus ex machina*, "the god from the machine," eventually became a standard reference to any awkward, mechanical, or unconvincing means used by a playwright to resolve the plot.

The Athenians, it seems, also invented the theater ticket, a necessity since the number of people who desired entrance far exceeded the facility's seating capacity. Spectators were drawn from all classes of the population (although slaves may have been excluded sometimes). Even many poor people became regulars after the democratic champion Pericles instituted a special government fund to subsidize their theater tokens about the year 450 B.C. The tokens, which resembled coins, were made of bronze, lead, ivory, bone, or terra-cotta. These audiences were lively. They hissed, groaned, booed, kicked their feet on the backs of their seats, or even threw vegetables when displeased with something onstage; and they applauded and cheered when they liked it.

AESCHYLUS AND THE TRILOGY

One major advantage Athenian audiences enjoyed over modern ones was the fact that at the time drama and theater were new institutions that existed nowhere else in the world. Theatrical conventions and ideas that today seem run-of-the-mill were, in fifth-century Athens, fresh and exciting. And it was in this stimulating, creative atmosphere that some of the greatest playwrights of all time worked their magic. Of the four fifth-century B.C. master playwrights, three—Aeschylus, Sophocles, and Euripides—produced mainly tragedies. The essence of tragedy, as these writers developed it, was the struggle of human beings to reconcile the existence of both good and evil. Noted scholar and translator Paul Roche puts it this way:

> The theme of all tragedy is the sadness of life and the universality of evil. The inference the Greeks drew from this was *not* that life was not worth living, but that because it *was* worth living the obstacles to it were worth overcoming. Tragedy is the story of our existence trying to rear its head above the general shambles.[2]

Early playwrights like Thespis and Phrynichus had set the basic form and tone of tragedy. But it was not until the early fifth century B.C. that Aeschylus, the first major theatrical innovator after Thespis, raised the art of tragedy to the level of great literature. Born about 525 B.C., as a young man Aeschylus witnessed Athens's steady rise toward political, military, and cultural greatness. And one of the epic events connected with that rise became the major theme of his *Persians,* written circa 472. The oldest surviving complete tragedy, the play depicts with a compelling sense of immediacy the sweeping Greek victory over Persia in the naval battle of Salamis in 480.

Of the ninety plays Aeschylus reportedly wrote, eighty-two titles are known, but only seven complete manuscripts survive. Besides the *Persians,* these are: *Seven Against Thebes* (written 467 B.C.); the *Oresteia,* a trilogy consisting of *Agamemnon, The Libation Bearers,* and *The Eumenides* (458); *The Suppliants* (ca. 463); and *Prometheus Bound* (ca. 460). Aeschylus won his first victory in the City Dionysia contests in 484 and went on to win twelve more times.

One of Aeschylus's great innovations was the introduction of a second actor. Until his time, following the tradition established by Thespis, playwrights made do with one actor; but this limited them to telling fairly simple stories with a few characters, which the lone actor attempted to portray using different masks. The addition of a second actor significantly expanded the story-telling potential, since it allowed the depiction of twice as many characters.

Aeschylus also broadened the scope of drama by employing the trilogy, a series of three plays related in plot and theme. By allowing a story to unfold in three successive plays, he was able to show in much more detail the evolution and impact of a concept such as justice, greed, or fate. For example, the three plays of the *Oresteia*, the only Greek trilogy that has survived complete, trace a repeating pattern of revenge and murder in the generations of the family of Agamemnon, King of Argos. At the climax of the third play, the violent cycle is broken when the goddess Athena intervenes.

SOPHOCLES AND EURIPIDES

The second great fifth-century B.C. tragedian was Sophocles, Aeschylus's junior by some thirty years. Born around 496 B.C. at Colonus, then a village just outside Athens's city walls, Sophocles hailed from a well-to-do family and so received an excellent education. He grew up to play important roles in public affairs, for a time holding the office of treasurer of the large federation of city-states Athens headed in the mid-to-late fifth century. But such accomplishments were inevitably overshadowed by his reputation as the most successful dramatist ever to present plays in the Theater of Dionysus. In his first victory in the City Dionysia, in 468 (for a play titled *Triptolemus*, now lost), he defeated Aeschylus; and he went on to win first prize at least eighteen times. (According to ancient sources, he sometimes won the second prize, but never the third.)

In retrospect, Sophocles' impact on the theater, in his own time and for all times, was nothing less than extraordinary. To begin with, his output of plays was huge—reportedly 123 in all. Unfortunately, only seven of these have survived: *Ajax* (ca. 447 B.C.), *Antigone* (ca. 441), *Oedipus the King* (ca. 429), *The Women of Trachis* (ca. 428), *Electra* (ca. 415), *Philoctetes* (ca. 409), and *Oedipus at Colonus* (406). Sophocles, a master of characterization, was the first playwright to use a third actor (and may also have employed a fourth toward the end of his career), which further increased the amount of character interaction in drama. The result of this development was a reduction in the importance of the chorus, the size of which he fixed at fifteen members.

Sophocles' plots generally revolve around central characters, whose personal flaws (often called "tragic" flaws) lead them to make mistakes that draw them and those around

them into crises and suffering. During the climax of a Sophoclean tragedy, the main character recognizes his or her er-
rors or crimes and accepts the punishment meted out by
society and/or the gods. The most famous example is the
plight of the title character in *Oedipus the King*. Through the
events of the story, Oedipus gradually learns that, unknow-
ingly, he has killed his own father and married his own
mother. Overwhelmed by the horror of these deeds, he accepts responsibility for them, blinds himself, and is doomed
to wander the countryside as a moral leper.

At the time that *Oedipus the King* first appeared before Athenian audiences, Euripides, the third giant of Greek tragedy, was
already in his fifties and had competed often with Sophocles in
the City Dionysia. Born in 485 B.C., the younger writer had his
first plays produced in 455. Of a total of some 88, nineteen have
survived, perhaps the most famous being *Medea* (431), *Hippolytus* (428), *Electra* (ca. 417–413), *The Trojan Women* (415),
Helen (412), and *The Bacchae* (405). Euripides won the dramatic
competitions only five times and was far less popular in his own
day than either Aeschylus or Sophocles. This was primarily because Euripides' plays often questioned traditional and widely
accepted social values. In exploring how humans shape their
own values and destinies, Euripides also depicted ordinary
people in highly realistic ways. Many Athenians saw this mode
of expression as too undignified for the tragic stage, which they
felt should show more heroic, larger-than-life people and
themes. Thus, Euripides was far ahead of his time, and later
scholars came to see him as the first playwright to deal with human problems in a modern way.

GREEK COMEDY

The tragic playwrights also wrote satyr-plays, which they
presented alongside their tragedies; however, though the underlying themes and morals of satyr-plays were usually of a
serious nature, their plots and overall tone were invariably
absurd and meant to make audiences laugh. Typically, they
were short; lampooned the mythical characters of the
tragedies; and featured obscene humor, both visual and verbal, performed in part by satyrs, with the mythical horse-
man, Silenus, frequently a leading character. The only
satyr-play that has survived complete is Euripides' *Cyclops*.

Out-and-out theatrical comedy was dominated in the last
half of the fifth-century B.C. by Aristophanes. The exact origins of comedy are uncertain; but it is likely that it developed

out of some of the same religious rituals that tragedy did. Most of the early Dionysian processions, including the dithyramb, were serious in nature. In time, however, some of these processions featured revelers dressed in animal costumes, particularly those depicting goats and horses. These worshipers in their satyr outfits danced, sang, and exchanged off-color jokes with onlookers. That such processions were one important source of comedy (*komoidia*) is supported by the term's root words—*komos,* meaning "revel," and *aeidein,* meaning "to sing." Another source of Greek comedy appears to have been mimes, essentially improvised comic skits originally performed informally in town squares. When actors began writing these skits down, they were performed at theaters, becoming the precursors of full-fledged comic plays.

Although comedies first appeared on the program at the City Dionysia in 501 B.C., they did not receive official recognition, including government support for production and prizes, until 487. The winner of the first comedic contest was the playwright Chionides, of whom almost nothing is known. The most creative period for Greek comedy, often referred to as the Old Comedy, lasted from about 450 to 404 B.C. The comic playwrights typically presented highly topical humor and poked fun at people of all walks of life, but especially politicians, generals, and other leaders. This constitutes one of the best illustrations of the extraordinary degree of freedom of speech (*parrhesia*) allowed under Athenian democracy. Such freedom, writes scholar James Butler, an expert on ancient theater, provided

> a license in language, situations, and stage portrayal difficult for us to realize fully, even today. It contained an incredible mixture of high [intellectual] and low [bawdy] comedy, satire, buffoonery, slapstick, verbal play, parody, allegory, metaphor, abuse, sex, caricature. . . singing, dancing, nudity, and vulgarity often in its crudest form.[5]

Aristophanes, who lived from about 445 to 388 B.C., was the undisputed master of the Old Comedy. Ancient writers attribute forty-four plays to him, but only eleven have survived: *Acharnians* (425), *Knights* (424), *Clouds* (423), *Wasps* (422), *Peace* (421), *Birds* (414), *Lysistrata* (411), *Women Celebrating the Thesmophoria* (411), *Frogs* (405), *Women in the Assembly* (392), and *Plutus* (382). Throughout his career, Aristophanes used biting satire to poke fun at the leaders and institutions of his day, usually depicting them in fantastic or absurd situations.

THE DEMISE AND LATER REDISCOVERY OF GREEK DRAMA

The theatrical reign of Aeschylus, Sophocles, Euripides, Aristophanes, and their contemporaries was short-lived. In 404 B.C., Athens went down to defeat in the conclusion of the horrific Peloponnesian War and the golden age of Athenian culture more or less ended. The City Dionysia and its competitions among playwrights continued, to be sure. But the era of extraordinary innovation and enormous creative output was over. The precise reasons that few, if any, more great Greek tragedies were written after the fifth century is unclear. Perhaps the playwrights felt that all that could be said in the tragic genre had already been said; or maybe audiences' tastes had changed in the wake of the great war's hardships and devastation.

Likewise, the comedies of the immediate post-war era were fewer, tamer, and less innovative and inspired. It is possible that the despair, depression, and disillusionment of the Athenians and other Greeks following the great war dampened both the comic playwrights' creative zeal and audiences' appreciation for humor. Later, from the 320s to about 260 B.C., the New Comedy, dominated by the popular Menander, thrived. On the one hand, it was more realistic and down to earth than the Old Comedy and just as popular; but it was also far tamer and less topical, satiric, and inventive.

Meanwhile, in Menander's day and long afterwards, some of the plays of the fifth-century B.C. masters continued to be performed. Unfortunately, many others were lost and with the disintegration of Greco-Roman civilization in late antiquity, Greek theaters went dark for many centuries. In time, however, the few surviving works of these masters were rediscovered and staged anew, awing and delighting modern generations, who saw in them a transcending universality and a literary quality never surpassed. Indisputably, this handful of gifted individuals had managed to create, in a stroke, the model for great drama and theater for all times.

NOTES

1. Aristotle, *Poetics* 4.10–13, in Richard McKeon, ed., *Introduction to Aristotle.* New York: Random House, 1947, p. 30.
2. Paul Roche, trans., *The Orestes Plays of Aeschylus.* New York: New American Library, 1962, p. xvii.
3. James H. Butler, *The Theater and Drama of Greece and Rome.* San Francisco: Chandler Publishing, 1972, p. 20.

CHRONOLOGY

534

The Athenians institute the great dramatics festival, the City Dionysia, dedicated to the fertility god, Dionysus; a poet named Thespis wins the competition and in the coming years establishes many of the standard conventions of the theater.

CA. 508

Athens establishes the world's first democracy.

490

The Athenians defeat an invading force of Persians on the plain of Marathon, northeast of Athens.

487

The Athenian government begins giving financial support for the production of comedies in the City Dionysia.

CA. 485

Euripides is born on the island of Salamis, a few miles south-west of Athens's urban center.

480

A united Greek naval force decisively defeats the Persians in the Bay of Salamis.

472

Aeschylus, the first great Athenian playwright, produces his play, *The Persians,* describing the victory at Salamis, in which he himself fought.

468

Another great playwright, Sophocles, wins his first victory in the City Dionysia contests.

461

A young politician named Pericles becomes the head of the democratic faction and Athens's most influential leader.

458

Aeschylus presents his mighty trilogy, the *Oresteia.*

455

Euripides first competes in the City Dionysia; his play, the *Peliades* (now lost), wins third prize.

CA. 450

Pericles establishes a special fund to provide the poor with theater tickets.

441

Euripides wins his first victory at the City Dionysia for a play whose title has since been lost.

438

The magnificent Parthenon temple, on the summit of Athens's central hill, the Acropolis, is dedicated to the city's patron goddess, Athena; Euripides produces *Alcestis.*

431

Euripides produces *Medea;* very soon afterward, the Peloponnesian War breaks out between Athens and Sparta and their respective leagues of allies.

430

Many Athenians die as a terrible plague strikes the city; Euripides produces the *Children of Heracles.*

429

The plague kills Pericles.

428

Euripides produces one of his greatest plays, *Hippolytus.*

421

The Peace of Nicias brings a temporary lull in the great war.

418

The war resumes with a vengeance.

CA. 417–413

Euripides produces *Electra.*

415

The Athenians launch a huge naval expedition against the Greek city of Syracuse, on the island of Sicily; Euripides produces *The Trojan Women.*

413

The Sicilian expedition ends in disaster as thousands of Athenians are killed or captured.

412

Euripides produces his play, *Helen,* about the legendary Greek woman whose great beauty supposedly ignited the Trojan War.

406

Euripides dies in Macedonia, where he had recently accepted an invitation to write at the local royal court; shortly afterward, Sophocles dies in Athens.

405

Euripides' plays, *The Bacchae* and *Iphigenia in Aulus,* are performed in Athens posthumously.

404

Athens is defeated in the great war, ending its cultural golden age.

FOR FURTHER RESEARCH

ABOUT EURIPIDES' LIFE AND WORKS

Aristotle, *Poetics,* in Robert Maynard Hutchins, ed., *The Works of Aristotle,* in *Great Books of the Western World Series.* Chicago: Encyclopedia Britannica, 1952.

Shirley A. Barlow, *The Imagery of Euripides: A Study in the Dramatic Use of Pictorial Language.* London: Methuen, 1971.

William N. Bates, *Euripides: A Student of Human Nature.* New York: Russell and Russell, 1969.

Michael Grant, *The Classical Greeks.* New York: Charles Scribner's Sons, 1989. Contains a biographical sketch of Euripides and his works.

L.H.G. Greenwood, *Aspects of Euripidean Tragedy.* New York: Russell and Russell, 1972.

Michael Halleran, *Stagecraft in Euripides.* Totowa, NJ: Barnes and Noble, 1985.

F.L. Lucas, *Euripides and His Influence.* New York: Cooper Square, 1963.

Siegfried Melchinger, *Euripides.* Trans. Samuel R. Rosenbaum. New York: Frederick Ungar, 1973.

Charles Segal, *Euripides and the Poetics of Sorrow.* Durham: Duke University Press, 1993.

Erich Segal, ed., *Euripides: A Collection of Critical Essays.* Englewood Cliffs, NJ: Prentice-Hall, 1968.

NOTEWORTHY TRANSLATIONS OF *MEDEA*
AND OTHER PLAYS BY EURIPIDES

Peter D. Arnott, trans. and ed., *Three Greek Plays for the Theater.* (Includes Euripides' *Medea* and *Cyclops,* and Aristophanes' *Frogs.*) Bloomington: Indiana University Press, 1961.

David Grene and Richmond Lattimore, eds., *Euripides III.* (Includes *Orestes, Iphigenia in Aulis, Electra, The Phoenician Women, The Bacchae.*) New York: Random House, 1959.

David Kovacs, trans., *Medea.* Cambridge, MA: Harvard University Press, 1994.

C.A. Robinson Jr., ed., *An Anthology of Greek Drama.* (Includes Euripides' *Medea* and *Hippolytus,* and assorted plays by Aeschylus, Sophocles, and Aristophanes.) New York: Holt, Rinehart and Winston, 1960.

David R. Slavitt and Palmer Bowie, eds., *Euripides, 1.* (Includes *Medea, Hecuba, Andromache, The Bacchae.*) Philadelphia: University of Pennsylvania Press, 1998.

Philip Vellacott, trans., *Euripides: Medea and Other Plays.* (Includes *Hecuba, Electra, Heracles.*) New York: Penguin Books, 1963.

———, *Euripides:* The Bacchae *and Other Plays.* (Includes *Ion, The Women of Troy,* and *Helen.*) Baltimore: Penguin Books, 1954.

———, *Euripides:* Alcestis, Hippolytus, Iphigenia in Tauris. Baltimore: Penguin Books, 1953.

Rex Warner, trans., *Three Great Plays of Euripides.* (Includes *Medea, Hippolytus, Helen.*) New York: New American Library, 1958.

ANCIENT GREEK DRAMA, THEATER, AND LITERATURE

James T. Allen, *Stage Antiquities of the Greeks and Romans and Their Influence.* New York: Cooper Square Publishers, 1963.

H.C. Baldry, *The Greek Tragic Theater.* New York: W.W. Norton, 1971.

C.M. Bowra, *Ancient Greek Literature.* New York: Oxford University Press, 1960.

James H. Butler, *The Theater and Drama of Greece and Rome.* San Francisco: Chandler Publishing, 1972.

Lionel Casson, *Masters of Ancient Comedy.* New York: Macmillan, 1960.

John Ferguson, *A Companion to Greek Tragedy.* Austin: University of Texas Press, 1972.

Moses Hadas, ed., *The Complete Plays of Aristophanes.* New York: Bantam Books, 1962.

Karelisa V. Hartigan, *Greek Tragedy on the American Stage: Ancient Drama in the Commercial Theater, 1882–1994.* Westport, CT: Greenwood Press, 1995.

H.D.F. Kitto, *Greek Tragedy.* Garden City, NY: Doubleday, 1952.

———, *Form and Meaning in Drama: A Study of Six Greek Plays and of* Hamlet. London: Methuen, 1956.

Bernard Knox, *Backing Into the Future: The Classical Tradition and Its Renewal.* New York: W.W. Norton, 1994.

———, *Word and Action: Essays on the Ancient Theater.* Baltimore: Johns Hopkins University Press, 1979.

Jan Kott, *The Eating of the Gods: An Interpretation of Greek Tragedy.* Trans. Boleslaw Taborski. New York: Random House, 1973.

Albin Lesky, *Greek Tragedy.* New York: Barnes and Noble, 1967.

Peter Levi, *A History of Greek Literature.* New York: Penguin Books, 1985.

D.W. Lucas, *The Greek Tragic Poets.* New York: W.W. Norton, 1959.

Don Nardo, ed., *Readings on Sophocles' Antigone.* San Diego: Greenhaven Press, 1999.

———, *Greek and Roman Theater.* San Diego: Lucent Books, 1995.

———, ed., *Greek Drama.* San Diego: Greenhaven Press, 2000.

Gilbert Norwood, *Greek Tragedy.* New York: Hill and Wang, 1960.

Arthur Pickard-Cambridge, *The Dramatic Festivals of Athens.* Oxford: Oxford University Press, 1968.

Meyer Reinhold, *Classical Drama, Greek and Roman.* Woodbury, NY: Barron's, 1959.

Jon Solomon, *The Ancient World in the Cinema.* New York: A.S. Barnes and Company, 1978.

ANCIENT GREEK HISTORY, SOCIETY, AND CULTURE

Lesley Adkins and Roy A. Adkins, *Handbook to Life in Ancient Greece.* New York: Facts On File, 1997.

Sue Blundell, *Women in Ancient Greece.* Cambridge, MA: Harvard University Press, 1995.

C.M. Bowra, *The Greek Experience.* New York: New American Library, 1957.

Eva Cantarella, *Pandora's Daughters: The Role and Status of Women in Greek and Roman Antiquity.* Baltimore: Johns Hopkins University Press, 1987.

E.R. Dodds, *The Greeks and the Irrational.* Berkeley: University of California Press, 1951.

Michael Grant, *Myths of the Greeks and Romans.* New York: New American Library, 1962.

Edith Hamilton, *The Greek Way to Western Civilization.* New York: New American Library, 1942.

———, *Mythology.* New York: New American Library, 1942.

Victor D. Hanson, *The Western Way of War: Infantry Battle in Classical Greece.* New York: Oxford University Press, 1989.

Victor D. Hanson and John Heath, *Who Killed Homer? The Demise of Classical Education and the Recovery of Greek Wisdom.* New York: Free Press, 1998.

Werner Jaeger, *Paideia: The Ideals of Greek Culture.* 3 vols. Trans. Gilbert Highet. New York: Oxford University Press, 1965.

Joint Association of Classical Teachers, *The World of Athens: An Introduction to Classical Athenian Culture.* New York: Cambridge University Press, 1984.

Robert B. Kebric, *Greek People.* Mountain View, CA: Mayfield Publishing, 1997.

Thomas R. Martin, *Ancient Greece: From Prehistoric to Hellenistic Times.* New Haven: Yale University Press, 1996.

Mark P.O. Morford and Robert J. Lenardon, *Classical Mythology.* New York: Longman, 1977.

Don Nardo, *The Age of Pericles.* San Diego: Lucent Books, 1996.

———, *The Decline and Fall of Ancient Greece.* San Diego: Greenhaven Press, 2000.

———, *Greek and Roman Mythology.* San Diego: Lucent Books, 1998.

———, *Greek and Roman Science.* San Diego: Lucent Books, 1997.

———, *Greek and Roman Sport.* San Diego: Lucent Books, 1999.

———, *Leaders of Ancient Greece.* San Diego: Lucent Books, 1999.

———, *Life in Ancient Athens.* San Diego: Lucent Books, 2000.

———, *The Parthenon.* San Diego: Lucent Books, 1999.

———, *The Trial of Socrates.* San Diego: Lucent Books, 1997.

Sarah B. Pomeroy, *Goddesses, Whores, Wives, and Slaves: Women in Classical Antiquity.* New York: Shocken Books, 1995.

Ian Scott-Kilvert, trans., *The Rise and Fall of Athens: Nine Greek Lives by Plutarch.* New York: Penguin Books, 1960.

Nigel Spivey, *Greek Art.* London: Phaidon Press, 1997.

Alfred Zimmern, *The Greek Commonwealth.* New York: Modern Library, 1931.

INDEX